**Healthy Recipes for Toddlers to Teens**

# Tarla Dalal

India's #1 Cookery Author

**S&C**
**SANJAY & CO.**
MUMBAI

# Other Books *by* Tarla Dalal

## INDIAN COOKING
- Tava Cooking
- Rotis & Subzis
- Desi Khana
- The Complete Gujarati Cook Book
- Mithai
- Chaat
- Achaar aur Parathe
- The Rajasthani Cookbook
- Swadisht Subzian
- Punjabi Khana `New`

## WESTERN COOKING
- The Complete Italian Cookbook
- The Chocolate Cookbook
- Eggless Desserts
- Mocktails & Snacks
- Soups & Salads
- Mexican Cooking
- Chinese Cooking
- Easy Chinese Cooking
- Thai Cooking
- Sizzlers & Barbeque

## MINI SERIES
- Idlis & Dosas
- Cooking under 10 minutes
- Pizzas and Pasta
- Fun Food for Children
- Roz Ka Khana
- Microwave - Desi Khana
- Paneer
- Parathas
- Chawal
- Dals
- Sandwiches
- Quick Cooking
- Curries & Kadhis
- Chinese Recipes
- Jain Desi Khana
- 7 Dinner Menus
- Jain International Recipes
- Punjabi Subzis
- Corn
- Microwave Subzis
- Baked Dishes
- Stir-Fry
- Potatoes `New`
- Recipes Using Leftovers `New`
- Noodles `New`
- Lebenese `New`

## TOTAL HEALTH
- Low Calorie Healthy Cooking
- Pregnancy Cookbook
- Baby and Toddler Cookbook
- Cooking with 1 Teaspoon of Oil
- Home Remedies
- Delicious Diabetic Recipes
- Fast Foods Made Healthy
- Healthy Soups & Salads
- Healthy Breakfast
- Calcium Rich Recipes
- Healthy Heart Cook Book
- Forever Young Diet
- Healthy Snacks
- Iron Rich Recipes
- Healthy Juices
- Low Cholesterol Recipes
- Good Food for Diabetes
- Healthy Subzis
- Healthy Snacks for Kids
- High Blood Pressure Cook Book
- Low Calorie Sweets
- Nutritious Recipes for Pregnancy
- Diabetic Snacks
- Zero Oil Rotis & Subzis `New`
- Zero Oil Soups, Salads & Snacks `New`
- Zero Oil Dal-Chawal `New`
- Acidity Cookbook `New`
- Soya Rotis & Subzis `New`

## GENERAL COOKING
- Exciting Vegetarian Cooking
- Microwave Recipes
- Saatvik Khana
- The Pleasures of Vegetarian Cooking
- The Delights of Vegetarian Cooking
- The Joys of Vegetarian Cooking
- Cooking with Kids
- Snacks Under 10 Minutes
- Ice-creams & Frozen Desserts
- Desserts Under 10 Minutes
- Entertaining
- Microwave Snacks & Desserts

First Printing : 2007

ISBN : 978-8-189491-56-7

## Price Rs. 250/-

Published & distributed by
**SANJAY & COMPANY**

A-1, 353 Shah & Nahar Industrial Estate, Dhanraj Mill Compound, Lower Parel (W), Mumbai 400 013, INDIA.
Tel: ( 91-22 ) 2496 8068  /  Fax: ( 91-22 ) 2496 5876  /  Email: sanjay@tarladalal.com  /  Website: www.tarladalal.com

"Tarla Dalal" is also a registered trademark owned by Sanjay & Co.

Copyright © **Sanjay & Co.**

**ALL RIGHTS RESERVED WITH THE PUBLISHERS**
No portion of this book shall be reproduced, stored in retrieval system or transmitted by any means, electronic, mechanical, photocopying, recording or otherwise, without the written permission of the publishers.

**Disclaimer**
While every precaution has been taken in the preparation of this book, the publishers and the author assume no responsibility for errors or omissions. Neither is any liability assumed for damages resulting from the use of information contained herein.

### UK and USA customers can call us on :
UK : 02080029533  •  USA : 213-634-1406
For books, Membership on **tarladalal.com**, Subscription for **Cooking & More** and Recipe queries
**Timing :** 9.30 a.m. to 7.00 p.m. (IST), from Monday to Saturday
*Local call charges applicable*

| **Recipe Research & Production Design**<br>Arati Fedane<br>Kunal Patil<br>Pragnesh Joshi | **Nutritionist**<br>Nisha Katira<br>Sapna Kamdar<br><br>**Crockery Courtesy**<br>HomeStop. | **Photography**<br>Payal Choksi<br><br><br>**Typesetting**<br>Adityas Enterprises | **Printed by**<br>Minal Sales Agencies, Mumbai<br><br><br>**Design**<br>Satyamangal Rege |
|---|---|---|---|

# Introduction

"Merry go round the mulberry bush, the mulberry bush, the mulberry bush!" That's how kids should be throughout the day... merrily going about their daily tasks, academics, games and what not, full of spirit! Punctuate their days with healthy snacks and meals and be assured that their activities are not punctuated with cumbersome coughs and sneezes and tiredness! Most mothers think *"fatter the child, healthier he is"* and thrust fatty foods down their throats just for the sake of it. Contrary to this is the fact that a child can be called healthy when he is active, free from diseases, infections and is growing well (as per his age). For this, mothers need to be aware of the nutritious benefits of various foods and make sure to serve them fun, filling and healthy foods throughout the day.

My book, *"Growing Kids Cookbook"* is an effort to help you in this task. Divided in **5 sections and comprising of 50 delicious and visually appealing recipes**, this book explains the importance of nutrition during the formative years and details of each nutrient. Besides recipes, we have also included **some fun and learn activities** for your kids to help him develop motor skills, coordination, and learn more about food and nutrients. Find answers to all these activities on page 96.

Growing kids need a double dose of energy and calorie-dense food provides the required energy and helps kick-start their day. However excess consumption can take longer to digest, cause dental caries, and most importantly add extra kilos! The first section of this book, called *"Run, Run, All Day"*, comprises of recipes that are made using carbohydrate rich foods along with moderate amounts of fat.

For kids to grow physically and to build a healthy body structure, they require nutrients like protein, calcium, phosphorous, magnesium etc. The section *"My Bones... Strongest"* is full of recipes that are rich in such nutrients. As kids go to school and interact with many others, they tend to contract colds and other contagious infections quite easily if their immune system is not strong enough. *"No More Colds"* section includes foods that are rich in nutrients like vitamins A, C and E, zinc and selenium that boost your children's immune power.

*"Fibre Rich Recipes"* is a vital section that provides you with recipes full of fibre to ensure easy digestion. And finally, last but most important, the section titled *"I Scored the Highest"* comprises of recipes that enhance brain power and soothe exam jitters... This section includes recipes rich in nutrients like carbohydrates, protein, fat, B-complex vitamins, zinc, iron and calcium.

Overall, this book has been planned so as to ensure the holistic good health of your children, not just today but in the future too! Make more and more of these healthy delicacies for your little one with lots and lots of love, from you and from me as well!

Warm regards,

# Contents

## RUN, RUN, ALL DAY
1. Apricot Orange Cookies ............................................................. 11
2. Golzeme ................................................................................... 12
3. Nutritious Bites ........................................................................ 14
4. Sugarcane Sorbet .................................................................... 14
5. Vegetable Pasta ....................................................................... 16
6. Mango Soya Milkshake ............................................................ 16
7. Whole Wheat Bread Cones with Potato and Mint Filling ........ 18
8. Mini Banana Folders ................................................................ 20
9. Quick Tawa Rice ...................................................................... 21
10. Corn Parathas .......................................................................... 22

## MY BONES...STRONGEST!
1. Khatta Meetha Chana Chaat ................................................... 26
2. Muesli Chocolate Rocks .......................................................... 28
3. Nutritious Noodles .................................................................. 30
4. Potato Zucchini Bake ............................................................... 32
5. Almond Til Chikki .................................................................... 33
6. Apricot and Walnut Pancakes with Orange Sauce ................. 34
7. Burger ...................................................................................... 36
8. Rajma, Spinach and Cheese Triangles .................................... 38
9. Stir-fried Vegetable Noodles ................................................... 40
10. Fruity Yoghurt ......................................................................... 42

## NO MORE COLDS
1. Veggie-Mayo Rolls ................................................................... 46
2. Pasta Salad .............................................................................. 48
3. Sunshine Boost ........................................................................ 48
4. Cheesy Corn and Spinach Pizza .............................................. 50

| 5. | Pineapple Stir-fry | 52 |
| 6. | Fruit Lollies | 54 |
| 7. | Cheese and Broccoli Tikkis | 56 |
| 8. | Lettuce Spoons | 58 |
| 9. | Walnut Fudge Fingers | 59 |
| 10. | Fruity Sandesh | 60 |

## FIBRE RICH RECIPES

| 1. | Green Peas and Paneer Mini Parathas | 64 |
| 2. | Papaya Pineapple Juice | 64 |
| 3. | Merry Macaroni | 66 |
| 4. | Kashmiri Fresh Fruit Rice | 67 |
| 5. | Toasted Stuffed Chapatis | 68 |
| 6. | Mini Mixed Vegetable Turnovers | 70 |
| 7. | Oats Pineapple Sheera | 70 |
| 8. | Cheese Chilli Frisbees | 72 |
| 9. | Apple and Cheese Toasts | 72 |
| 10. | Green Pea and Corn Bhel | 74 |

## "I SCORED THE HIGHEST"

| 1. | Chana Spinach Rice | 79 |
| 2. | Almond Sheera | 80 |
| 3. | Mini Raisin Muffins | 82 |
| 4. | Vegetable Houses | 84 |
| 5. | Muesli Coated Fruits | 86 |
| 6. | Spinach Malfati | 88 |
| 7. | Pulse Appe | 90 |
| 8. | Paneer Papad Kurkure | 92 |
| 9. | Labneh with Crispy Vegetables | 94 |
| 10. | Orange Banana Smoothie | 95 |

# A-Z building blocks of good health

*A for apple, B for bananas, C for carrots, D for dairy products... there is no dearth of healthy foodstuffs, but how well they are combined, prepared and served to kids in a form they will like is of great importance!*

*The food you give your children forms the building blocks for their body, and has a lasting influence on total well-being, physical and mental health, today and tomorrow. They prevent immediate health problems such as iron deficiency anaemia, obesity, eating disorders and dental caries, besides long-term health problems such as coronary heart disease, cancer and stroke.*

- **A**lways have a heavy and healthy breakfast
- **B**e physically active
- **C**urtail intake of processed foods like bread, biscuits, wafers etc.
- Get vitamin **D** from sunlight and build bones
- Avoid unnecessary **E**xam anxiety
- Chew your **F**ood properly
- **G**o greens everyday
- **H**aul back chocolate and cocoa
- **I**ncrease intake of fruits and fight diseases
- Restrict **J**unk foods
- **K**nock out excessive salt consumption
- Eat **L**oads of sprouts

**M**aintain good health

**N**ourish your body with at least 8-10 glasses of water daily

Don't **O**verfeed your child

**P**lan short and frequent meals

**Q**uit aerated drinks

**R**estrict intake of fried foods

**S**nack smartly

**T**urn to dairy products

Make **U**se of a variety of veggies

**V**ariety in meals

**W**atch your weight

Avoid **X**cess of sugary foods

Don't **Y**earn for tea and coffee

**Z**ip up your diet with whole grains and cereals

# Run, Run, All Day

As the years pass, right from infancy to pre-school age and till the child enters the teenage, there is a rapid growth and development taking place. Also children are always curious to know and learn new things around them, which keep them occupied with multifarious activities. All these require a good amount of energy (in the form of glucose) and an extra dose of nutrients. A well-balanced diet made up of all five food groups viz. cereals and pulses, milk and milk products, fruits and vegetables, fat and oil, fluids etc. will keep them fit to run all day long. Here is some know-how about the nutrients that can work this magic!

## Carbohydrate - the energy giver

Amongst all the nutrients that a child should consume, carbohydrate is the most vital nutrient and an important part of the diet because:

- Carbohydrate provides instant and major source of energy for a child's body and brain which keeps them active throughout the day. This is the reason your child requires four to five short and frequent meals comprising of carbohydrate rich foods, fruits, vegetables etc to keep the sugar level and energy levels optimum. However, remember not to overfeed your child as any excess carbohydrate than that required by the body gets converted to fat and is stored in the liver.
- Spare the protein from being used up for energy, allowing them to be used for the major role of tissue growth and maintenance.

## So which type of carbohydrates should you give your child and how much?

There are two major types of carbohydrates in foods: simple and complex.

- **Simple carbohydrates:** These are simple sugar which are ready to be absorbed easily. Foods like table sugar, honey, milk and fruits (mangoes, *chickoo*, banana etc) are sources of simple carbohydrates. It is recommended by experts to consume a bulk of simple carbohydrates by way of milk and fruits as they contain vitamins, fibre and minerals which is otherwise lacking in sugar.

➤ **Complex carbohydrates:** These include starches which take longer time to digest. Cereals like wheat, brown rice, oats, rice, *jowar*, *bajra*, refined flour (*maida*) and their products like pasta, noodles, biscuits, bread etc. Amongst these foods, refined flour and its products are devoid of fibre hence it is advisable to restrict its intake or have it in restricted quantity in combination with loads of vegetables. Instead include more of whole grains and cereals in their diet as they help curb the intake of unnecessary calories (a major cause of childhood obesity), prevent tooth decays and help to introduce the children to a horde of foods thereby offering variety in their diet.

## Fats a concentrated source of energy

To meet your child's increased calorie requirements, carbohydrates alone may not help. Fat too are needed, for the following reasons:

➤ Fat is an important nutrient that provides ample energy, i.e., 9 kcal per gm.

➤ It helps in the absorption and utilisation of fat-soluble vitamins like A, D, E and K.

➤ It insulates your child's body from cold, and provide cushioning and protection to vital organs.

➤ It also helps to keep your child's immune system functioning at its best.

## Types of fats?

Fats can be categorized as visible fat and invisible fat.

➤ **Visible fats** include oil, butter, ghee, margarine etc. that are added to the foods while cooking.

➤ **Invisible fats** are those that are naturally present in foods like cereals, pulses, nuts, meat, milk and milk products etc.

## How should I give fat to my child and does quantity matter?

It is true the that visible fats like oil and ghee play an important role in food preparation by enhancing food flavour, improving texture, and making the food palatable. No kid will ever say no to French fries, chips, deep fried *tikkis* etc., however as a parent it is your duty to set the limits.

It is true that growing kids need some visible fat, but excessive intake can contribute to weight gain and other illnesses that occur as they age, like heart problems, diabetes etc. This does not mean you should totally prevent your children from consuming fatty foods or foods that they like; just restrict the quantity remember moderation is the key. Hence give them small portions of the fatty foods once in 15 days. As well as use oil in moderation in your daily cooking. On the other hand, invisible fats like nuts viz. cashewnuts, almonds, coconut etc. are no doubt a pack of energy and nutrients but they also abound of saturated fats. Hence benefit from them by consuming in limited quantities and munching a packetful of them daily.

## *In this section...*

Recipes are energy dense and filling enough to keep your child going till evening. I have included foods that provide a good amount of carbohydrates like whole wheat flour, rice, vegetables like potatoes, fruits like mangoes and banana, whole wheat bread, sugarcane, pasta etc., and these are cooked in moderate amounts of fat. There are popular and innovative recipes like **Golzeme,** *page 12,* **Nutritious Bites,** *page 14,* **Whole Wheat Bread Cones with Potato and Mint Filling,** *page 18* etc., that are filling, nutritious, and tasty so that kids will certainly relish them. Giving refined foods like pasta, noodles, bread, maida etc. to your child once in a while is not bad if combined with lots of vegetables like I have done in **Apricot Orange Cookies,** *page 11,* and **Vegetable Pasta,** *page 16.* Kids may avoid eating whole fruits, hence make **Mango Soya Milkshake,** *page 16* or **Mini Banana Folders,** *page 20,* to include them in their diet. Readily available candy bars, lollies and energy bars can be fattening as they are loaded with fat and sugar; so replace them with healthy **Sugarcane Sorbet,** *page 14,* and watch your child relish every sip of it.

# Apricot Orange Cookies

Apricots and oranges come together in an exciting form that will make your kids go, "WOW!" And of course, cashewnuts add a crunch that no child can resist.

Nutritive values per cookie
Energy: 81 kcal
Carbohydrate: 7.3 gm
Fat: 5.2 gm

**Preparation Time:** 25 minutes. **Cooking Time:** Nil. **Makes 16 cookies.**
**Baking Temperature:** 160ºC (320ºF). **Baking Time:** 25 to 30 minutes.

¾ cup whole wheat flour (*gehun ka atta*)
½ cup butter
¼ cup powdered sugar
¼ tsp baking powder
¼ tsp soda-bi-carb
1½ tbsp dried chopped apricots (*kuumani / jardalu*)
1½ tbsp chopped cashewnuts (*kaju*)
2 tsp orange flavoured drink mix
⅓ cup milk
½ tsp butter for greasing

1. Combine all the ingredients together in a bowl and whisk to get a soft dough.
2. Pour into a piping bag fitted with a large star nozzle.
3. Pipe out 37 mm (1½") diameter cookies on to a greased baking tray.
4. Bake in a pre-heated oven at 160ºC (320ºF) for 20 to 25 minutes or till the cookies are golden brown in colour.
5. Cool completely and store in an air-tight container.

# Golzeme

A secret portion from Turkey to make sure your kids bubble with energy! Both wholesome and nutritious, this is an ideal recipe for breakfast.

Nutritive values per *golzeme*
Energy: 158 kcal
Protein: 5.5 gm
Fat: 7.3 gm

Preparation Time: 1 hour.    Cooking Time: 20 minutes.    Makes 8 *golzeme*.

**For the *rotis***
1 cup plain flour *(maida)*
¼ cup rice flour *(chawal ka atta)*
Salt to taste

**For the stuffing**
1 cup boiled and grated potatoes (90% cooked)
1 cup chopped spinach *(puluk)*
1 cup crumbled *paneer* (cottage cheese)
Dry red chilli flakes to taste
Salt to taste
8 tbsp grated mozzarella cheese

**Other ingredients**
Whole wheat flour *(gehun ka atta)* for rolling
1 tbsp olive oil / any oil for cooking

**For the *rotis***
1. Combine together all the ingredients in a bowl and knead to a soft, smooth dough using hot water as required.
2. Keep aside covered with a wet muslin cloth for one hour.
3. Knead again and divide the dough into 8 equal portions. Keep aside.

**How to proceed**
1. Divide the stuffing into 8 equal portions and keep aside.
2. Roll out each portion of the dough into a circle of 175 mm. (7") diameter.
3. Place a circle on a flat surface, spread 2 tbsp of potatoes, then 2 tbsp of spinach and finally 2 tbsp of *paneer* on one half of the circle.
4. Sprinkle chilli flakes and salt over it.
5. Top with 1 tbsp of mozzarella cheese, fold into a semi-circle and press gently.
6. Cook on a non-stick *tava* (griddle) using a little oil till brown spots appear on both the sides.
7. Cut into 4 equal pieces and serve immediately.
8. Repeat with the remaining dough and stuffing to make 7 more *golzeme*.

**Other *golzeme* ideas :**
*You can use a variety of stuffings as follows*
1. Grated potato, cheese and pepper.
2. Grated carrots and *paneer*.
3. Grated cauliflower and chopped onions.
4. Only lots of cheese.
5. Crumbled *paneer* and green *chutney* mix.

# Nutritious Bites

Just a piece of this energy bar, at any time of the day, is enough to recharge your child and continue being as bouncy as ever! The chosen flours and jaggery provide ample energy and carbohydrates!

Nutritive values per piece
Energy: 181 kcal
Carbohydrate: 20.5 gm
Fat: 9.4 gm

**Preparation Time: 10 minutes.   Cooking Time: 20 minutes.   Makes 10 pieces.**

2½ tbsp ghee
⅓ cup whole wheat flour (*gehun ka atta*)
¼ cup soya flour
2 tbsp *ragi / nachni* (red millet) flour
⅓ cup chopped jaggery (*gur*)
1 tsp sliced almonds (*badam*)
1 tbsp roasted poppy seeds (*khus-khus*)

1. Heat the ghee in a non-stick pan, add the wheat flour and roast on a slow flame while stirring continuously till it turns slightly brown in colour.
2. Add the soya flour and *ragi* flour and roast on a slow flame till it turns golden brown in colour while still stirring continuously.
3. Remove from the flame, add the jaggery and mix well. Stir continuously till the jaggery melts.
4. Pour the mixture into a greased *thali* and spread it evenly using a spatula.
5. When slightly cool, cut it into equal pieces of desired shapes using different moulds or cookie cutters as shown in the picture.
6. Cover the sides by sticking poppy seeds on them.

**Handy tip:** You could also decorate these with some icing to make them more attractive as shown in the picture.

# Sugarcane Sorbet

Why go for readymade ice-creams or lollies that provide only calories and no nutrients? Treat your child to sugarcane, a natural source of carbohydrates, in this interesting way!

Nutritive values per serving
Energy: 204 kcal
Carbohydrate: 48.8 gm
Fat: 0.6 gm

**Preparation Time: 10 minutes.   Cooking Time: Nil.   Serves 4.**

6 cups sugarcane juice
6 tbsp sugar
Juice of ½ lemon
2 to 3 drops of ginger juice (optional)

1. Combine all the ingredients in a bowl and mix well till the sugar dissolves.
2. Pour into a shallow container, cover and freeze till it is set (approx. 4 to 6 hours).
3. Transfer to a mixer and blend till slushy.
4. Spoon it into 4 individual glasses and serve immediately.

# Vegetable Pasta

Kids love all things colourful! That is what made me choose colourful veggies for this dish, and what's better is that the veggies will also boost your kids' nutrient meter for the day!

Nutritive values per serving
Energy: 197 kcal
Carbohydrate: 24.8 gm
Fat: 7.0 gm

Preparation Time: 10 minutes.   Cooking Time: 10 minutes.   Serves 4.

2 tsp butter
2 tsp finely chopped garlic
¼ cup chopped onions
¼ cup chopped capsicum
¼ cup broccoli florets, blanched
¼ cup chopped carrots, blanched
½ cup chopped tomatoes
½ tsp finely chopped green chillies (optional)
2 cups boiled penne pasta
3 tbsp grated mozzarella cheese
¾ cup milk

Salt to taste

1. Heat the butter in a non-stick pan, add the garlic, onions and capsicum and sauté for 3 to 4 minutes while stirring continuously.
2. Add the broccoli, carrots, tomatoes, green chillies and sauté again for 2 to 3 minutes.
3. Add the pasta, cheese, milk and salt and mix well. Cook for another 3 to 4 minutes or till the cheese melts. Serve hot.

# Mango Soya Milkshake

Plain soya milk may be boring, but your kids just can't resist it when blended with mango pulp. Believe me; they'll come asking for more!

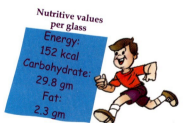

Nutritive values per glass
Energy: 152 kcal
Carbohydrate: 29.8 gm
Fat: 2.3 gm

Preparation Time: 10 minutes.   Cooking Time: Nil.   Makes 2 glasses.

1 cup of unsweetened soya milk
¾ cup mango pulp, refer handy tip
1½ tbsp sugar
4-5 ice-cubes, crushed
2 tbsp chopped mangoes for the garnish

1. Combine all the ingredients together in a mixer and blend till smooth. Refrigerate to chill.
2. Pour into individual glasses and serve chilled garnished with mangoes.

**Handy tip:** 1 cup of chopped mangoes gives approximately ¾ cup of mango pulp.

# Whole Wheat Bread Cones with Potato and Mint Filling

Children love finger foods... they are hep! Whole wheat bread cones served with the all-time favourite potato is sure to rock their snack time, in a healthy way.

Nutritive values per cone
Energy: 126 kcal
Carbohydrate: 19.9 gm
Fat: 3.9 gm

Preparation Time: 20 minutes.   Cooking Time: 20 minutes.   Makes 6 cones.
Baking Temperature: 180°C (360°F).   Baking Time: 15 to 17 minutes.

**For the cones**
1 tsp butter for greasing
6 whole wheat bread slices

**For the potato and mint filling**
2 tsp oil
½ tsp cumin seeds (*jeera*)
½ cup boiled and chopped potatoes
¼ cup boiled sweet corn kernels (*makai ke dane*)
1 tbsp finely chopped mint leaves (*phudina*)
1 tbsp finely chopped coriander (*dhania*)
2 tbsp milk
1 tbsp grated mozzarella cheese
Salt to taste

**Other ingredients**
2 tbsp grated mozzarella cheese for the topping
2 tbsp tomato ketchup for serving

**For the cones**
1. Remove the crusts from the bread slices.
2. Wrap the bread slices in a muslin cloth and steam them for 5 to 7 minutes in a pressure cooker.
3. Roll out each slice using a rolling pin.
4. Shape each slice to make a cone and secure the cone inserting a toothpick.
5. Bake in a pre-heated oven at 180°C (360°F) for 4 to 5 minute and keep aside.

**For the potato and mint filling**
1. Heat the oil in a non-stick pan and add the cumin seeds.
2. When the seeds crackle, add the potatoes, corn, mint leaves and coriander and mix well.
3. Add the milk, cheese and salt, mix well and cook for 2 to 3 minutes.
4. Remove from the flame and divide the mixture into 6 equal portions. Keep aside.

**How to proceed**
1. Spoon a portion of the filling mixture into each bread cone.
2. Sprinkle a tsp of cheese on top of each cone and bake in a pre-heated oven at 180°C (360°F) for 8 to 10 minutes or till the cones turn light brown in colour and crisp.

Serve immediately with tomato ketchup.

**Handy tip:** The bread slices should be absolutely fresh, else the cones will crack.

# Mini Banana Folders

Whole wheat rotis stuffed with sweet, carbohydrate rich bananas. Doubt not that the kids will go bananas over this nutritious and energising breakfast that will satisfy both their hunger pangs and sweet tooth!

Nutritive values per folder
Energy: 122 kcal
Carbohydrate: 22.8 gm
Fat: 2.8 gm

Preparation Time: 10 minutes.    Cooking Time: 25 minutes.    Makes 8 mini folders.

¾ cup whole wheat flour (*gehun ka atta*)
¾ cup finely chopped bananas
8 tsp orange marmalade
4 tsp sugar
1 tbsp plain flour (*maida*) mixed with 2 tbsp water
Oil for deep-frying

1. Take the wheat flour in a bowl and knead into a soft, smooth dough using enough water. Keep aside.
2. Divide the dough into 16 equal portions and roll out each portion into a thin 100 mm (4") square.
3. Cook each square on a non-stick pan on one side.
4. Place a square on a clean, flat surface with the cooked side facing up.
5. Apply a little flour paste and place another square on it taking care to leave the edges dry so that the edges separate when the folders are deep-fried.
6. Spread 1 tbsp of bananas evenly on one half and 1 tsp of the marmalade evenly over it.
7. Sprinkle ½ tsp of sugar and fold to make a triangle.
8. Heat the oil in a *kadhai* and deep-fry till it turns golden brown in colour.
9. Repeat with the remaining ingredients to make 7 more mini folders. Serve hot.

# Quick Tawa Rice

Your little ones will surely love this dish as it is both colourful and yummy! And you will love it too, because it is quick to make and easy to serve.

Nutritive values per serving
Energy: 192 kcal
Carbohydrate: 34.1 gm
Fat: 4.3 gm

Preparation Time: 10 minutes.     Cooking Time: 8-10 minutes.     Serves 4.

1 tbsp oil
½ cup finely chopped spring onions with the greens
2 tsp ginger-garlic paste
½ tsp chilli powder
¼ tsp turmeric powder (*haldi*)
¼ cup chopped capsicum
¼ cup chopped tomatoes
2 tbsp fresh curds (*dahi*)
½ cup boiled *kabuli chana* (chick peas)
¼ cup boiled green peas
3 cups cooked rice
Salt to taste

1. Heat the oil in a non-stick pan, add the spring onions and sauté for 1 minute.
2. Add the ginger-garlic paste and again sauté for a few seconds.
3. Add the chilli powder, turmeric powder, capsicum, tomatoes and curds and cook for 5 minutes while stirring continuously.
4. Add the *kabuli chana*, green peas, rice and salt, mix well and cook for another minute.
Serve hot.

# Corn Parathas

Parathas sure are filling, and will keep your child satisfied till the next meal. These parathas surely does solve your woes as well, because your child will consume the nutritious spinach that is masked in the dough!

**Nutritive values per *paratha***
Energy: 88 kcal
Carbohydrate: 9.2 gm
Fat: 4.7 gm

Preparation Time: 15 minutes.   Cooking Time: 20 minutes.   Makes 5 mini *parathas*.

½ cup whole wheat flour (*gehun ka atta*)
¼ cup coarsely crushed sweet corn kernels (*makai ke dane*)
¼ cup finely chopped spinach (*palak*)
¼ tsp finely chopped green chillies
Salt to taste
¼ tsp oil for kneading
whole wheat flour (*gehun ka atta*) for rolling
5 tsp grated mozzarella cheese
1 tbsp oil for cooking

1. Combine the wheat flour, corn, spinach, green chillies and salt in a bowl and knead to a soft, smooth dough using enough water. Keep aside for 5 minutes.
2. Knead again using oil and keep aside under a wet muslin cloth.
3. Divide the dough into 10 equal portions and roll each into 100 mm (4") thin *rotis* using little wheat flour.
4. Place a *roti* on a flat surface, sprinkle 1 tsp of cheese and spread it evenly.
5. Cover with another *roti* and press lightly.
6. Heat a non-stick pan and cook each *paratha* using little oil till brown spots appear on both the sides.
7. Repeat with the remaining ingredients to make 4 more *parathas*.
Serve immediately.

### Make the picture:
*Join the dots in the correct order to find the hidden picture.*

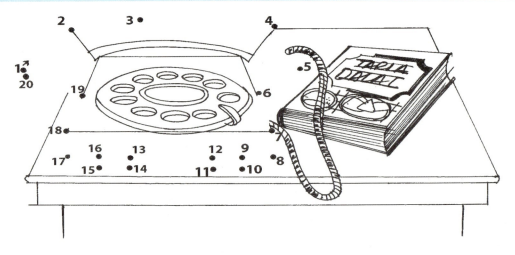

# My Bones…Strongest!

It is very easy for a mother to recognise how fast her child is growing… with or without the hints provided by clothes getting shorter or smaller! It is all an effect of the skeletal growth that occurs along with the bone and muscle development during these years. Your child's bones grow and develop till adulthood, but the childhood years are the foundation for stronger bones. This is the time when bones get calcified and stronger along with the increase in muscle mass that demands a constant supply of necessary nutrients like protein, calcium, phosphorous etc in the form of a healthy diet.

## Which nutrients work to make your child's bones stronger?

Nutrients like protein and calcium along with minerals like phosphorus, magnesium and vitamins C and D work hand in hand to make your child's bones stronger. So, let us explore more about these nutrients…

**PROTEIN:** Protein is vital for your child's bone health as:

- It is required for the formation of new bone cells and their growth.
- Any damage to the bone cell or tissue is repaired and maintained by protein.
- They help make haemoglobin, that carry oxygen and other nutrients throughout our body.
- They provide energy when carbohydrates and fat are deficient.

Protein is found in foods like milk and milk products like curds, *paneer*, cheese etc, non-vegetarian foods, eggs, cereals, pulses, *dals* and nuts. To benefit the most it is advisable to give a combination of foods to growing kids. Hence combine milk with a cereal to make porridge, or combine rice with *dal* to make *khichdi*.

**CALCIUM:** It is a mineral that aids building and strengthening of bones and teeth. During childhood there is a rapid formation of new bone cells and teeth enamel. When new cells are formed, calcium starts depositing on them thereby making them firmer and stronger. Hence, give required amount of calcium to your child by including milk and milk products (like curds, cheese and *paneer*), leafy vegetables (like spinach, fenugreek, cauliflower), broccoli, sesame seeds, *nachni*, asparagus, pulses (like soyabeans, *moong*, *matki*, sprouts etc.)

**VITAMIN C:**

- Aids calcium absorption from foods
- Maintains healthy bones, teeth and blood vessels
- Promotes healing of wounds and broken bones.

Include plenty of fresh fruits like oranges, sweet lime, pineapple, guava, amla and vegetables like capsicum, cabbage and broccoli and sprouts to get the required share of vitamin C.

## PHOSPHOROUS:
➤ Works with calcium to build strong bones and teeth by making it available to bone cells.
➤ Helps in bone metabolism process.

## MAGNESIUM:
➤ Helps in growth and development of bones.

*Eating a well balanced diet comprising all the five food groups is just enough to provide your child the necessary nutrients like phosphorous and magnesium.*

## VITAMIN D:
➤ Enhances calcium absorption.
➤ Aids in strengthening of bones and teeth.
➤ Keep muscles supple.

Vitamin D is found in most non-vegetarian foods; however our body can make its own when exposed to sunlight. Hence, expose your child to sunlight early in the morning to get a good share of vitamin D.

Along with a balanced diet, your child's daily routine should also include plenty of playtime. **"All work and no play" is more a reality now than ever before**. Even the healthiest of foods can be stored as fat if your child's day is all work and no play, turning him or her into a couch potato. Physical exercise helps children to be active throughout the day, improve coordination, grow tall, and eat better as well.

## *In this section...*

I have taken care to include all the sources of the above-mentioned nutrients. Recipes like **Potato Zucchini Bake,** *page 32* and **Fruity Yoghurt,** *page 42*, provide ample protein and calcium. Other sources like *chana, rajma,* vegetables are innovatively used in recipes like **Khatta Meetha Chana Chaat,** *page 26,* **Rajma, Spinach and Cheese Triangles,** *page 38* and **Stir-Fried Vegetable Noodle,** *page 40.*

I have modified recipes that are popular with kids like noodles, *chaat* and burger to make healthier versions using ingredients like vegetables, soyabeans, bulgur wheat etc. Nuts like almonds, walnuts, *til*, muesli etc. also are good sources of calcium and protein and are hence used to make kids-friendly recipes like **Muesli Chocolate Rocks,** *page 28,* **Almond Til Chikki,** *page 33,* **Apricot and Walnut Pancakes with Orange Sauce,** *page 34* . I have used moderate amounts of chocolate for making Muesli Chocolate Rocks to make them eat nutritious muesli, which they would not eat otherwise.

Make these recipes for your little ones and watch them growing faster and stronger.

# Khatta Meetha Chana Chaat

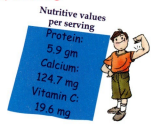

**Nutritive values per serving**
Protein: 5.9 gm
Calcium: 124.7 mg
Vitamin C: 19.6 mg

Sweet and sour, chatpata chaat... mom, you are gonna rise really high up your kid's popularity chart! This is a smart way to make your child consume protein and calcium rich kabuli chana and paneer, which might otherwise not seem too enticing.

Preparation Time: 20 minutes.    Cooking Time: 10 minutes.    Serves 4.

1 tbsp butter
½ tsp cumin seeds (*jeera*)
1 cup boiled *kabuli chana* (chick peas)
1 cup boiled, peeled and chopped potatoes
½ cup chopped *paneer* (cottage cheese)
½ cup chopped tomatoes
¼ cup *khatti-meethi chutney*, recipe below
Salt to taste
½ tsp lemon juice
2 tbsp chopped coriander (*dhania*)

**For the *khatti-meethi chutney***
1 tsp cumin seeds (*jeera*)
2 cups chopped mint leaves (*phudina*)
1 cup chopped coriander (*dhania*)
4 to 6 green chillies, roughly chopped
12 mm. (½") piece ginger
Juice of 1 to 2 lemons
2 tbsp sugar
½ tsp *chaat masala*

Salt to taste

**For the *khatti-meethi chutney***
1. Combine all the ingredients and blend in a mixer to a smooth paste using a little water if required.
2. Refrigerate and use as required.

**How to proceed**
1. Heat the butter in a non-stick pan and add the cumin seeds.
2. When the seeds crackle, add the *kabuli chana*, potatoes, *paneer* and tomatoes, mix well and cook for 1 minute.
3. Remove from the flame and keep aside to cool.
4. When cool, add the *khatti-meethi chutney*, salt, lemon juice and coriander and mix well.
Serve immediately.

## Pave a Path

*Help these animals to get their food by drawing a path in between the lines, without touching the borders. This activity helps in developing motor skills of your child.*

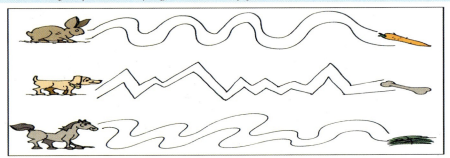

# Muesli Chocolate Rocks

Nutritious muesli is combined with luscious chocolate to make these crunchy and nutritious rocks! Each rock brims with protein and calcium making this a healthy alternative to sugar-laden candies that cause dental caries. What more can I say... this recipe rocks!

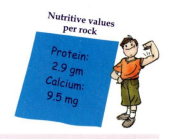

Nutritive values per rock
Protein: 2.9 gm
Calcium: 9.5 mg

Preparation Time: 10 minutes.    Cooking Time: 15 minutes.    Makes 16 rocks.

**For the muesli**
¼ cup quick rolled cooking oats
¼ cup cornflakes
2 tbsp chopped mixed nuts (cashewnuts, walnuts and almonds)
1 tsp wheat bran (*konda*)
2 tsp chopped raisins (*kismis*)
2 tsp castor sugar

**For the chocolate sauce**
¼ cup grated milk chocolate
2 tbsp grated dark chocolate

**For the muesli**
1. Combine the oats, cornflakes, nuts and wheat bran in a non-stick pan and lightly roast them over a slow flame for 5 to 7 minutes.
2. Cool completely, add the raisins and sugar and mix well. Keep aside.

**For the chocolate sauce**
1. Combine the milk chocolate and dark chocolate in a bowl.
2. Place the bowl on top of a double boiler, taking care to see that the base of the bowl is not in contact with the water in the double boiler.
3. Once the chocolate starts melting, stir continuously till the chocolate melts completely and resembles a smooth sauce.
4. Remove from the double boiler immediately and keep on stirring till it cools but not set. Keep aside.

**How to proceed**
1. Add the muesli to the melted chocolate and mix gently.
2. Divide it into 16 equal portions and spoon out each into grease-proof paper cups and allow to cool.
Serve immediately.

### Chef's Tip!
- If you do not have the time to make muesli, just buy a readymade muesli from the market.
- Fresh fruits like strawberries, bananas, peaches, oranges etc. and nuts can also be coated with chocolate instead of muesli for an exciting variation.

# Nutritious Noodles

Don't prevent your kids from eating their favourite foods; inject good health into them instead by adding the right ingredients. For example, use rice noodles instead of refined flour (maida) noodles and add healthy ingredients like veggies, sprouts, peanuts etc. By concocting healthier versions of their favourite dishes, your kids can have their way, and so can you!

**Nutritive values per serving**
Protein: 4.2 gm
Calcium: 26.6 mg
Vitamin C: 5.1 mg

Preparation Time: 10 minutes.    Cooking Time: 10 minutes.    Serves 4.

200 gm rice noodles (dried rice vermicelli)
1 tbsp oil
2 tsp garlic paste
1 small dry whole red chilli
¼ cup chopped spring onions (with greens)
¼ cup chopped French beans, blanched
¼ cup chopped carrots, blanched
¼ cup sliced mushrooms (*khumbh*), optional
1 stalk celery, finely chopped
¼ cup bean sprouts
¼ cup peanuts, roasted and chopped
2 tsp soya sauce
1 tsp sugar
1 tbsp lemon juice
Salt and freshly ground pepper to taste

1. Place the noodles in a large bowl.
2. Boil 1 litre of water with a little salt in a broad pan and pour it over the raw rice noodles. Cover and keep aside for 10 minutes or till the noodles are soft. Drain and keep aside.
3. Heat the oil in a non-stick pan, add the garlic paste, red chilli, spring onions, French beans, carrots, mushrooms and celery and sauté for 2 to 3 minutes.
4. Add the noodles, bean sprouts, peanuts, soya sauce, sugar, lemon juice, salt and pepper and toss well. Sprinkle 1 tbsp of water if required to moisten the noodles. Serve immediately.

## Oodles of Noodles

*Follow the noodles over and under using two coloured pens (blue for the boy and red for the girl) to see which kid gets which piece of cheese.*

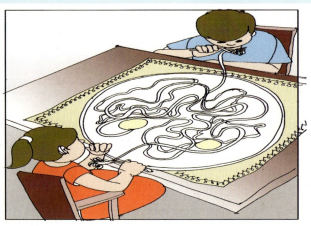

# Potato Zucchini Bake

Potato and cheese... both are hot favourites with kids! Cheese is high in protein and calcium, a perfect food for growing kids; however it is better to restrict its intake... no thanks to its high fat content. I have used mozzarella cheese instead of cooking cheese as its fat content is comparatively lower.

Nutritive values per serving
Protein: 2.9 gm
Calcium: 80.0 mg
Vitamin C: 19.8 mg

Preparation Time: 10 minutes. Cooking Time: 20 minutes. Serves 4.
Baking Temperature: 200°C (400°F). Baking Time: 25 minutes.

½ tsp butter for greasing
2 big potatoes, boiled, peeled and cut into thick slices
1½ tbsp cream
6 tbsp grated mozzarella cheese
Salt and freshly ground pepper to taste
½ tsp dried oregano
1 small zucchini, cut into thin slices
1 big tomato, cut into thin slices
2 tbsp tomato ketchup for serving

1. Grease a glass baking tray with butter and arrange the potato slices at the bottom in an even layer.
2. Put ½ tbsp of cream, 2 tbsp of cheese, salt, pepper and oregano over the potatoes.
3. Arrange the zucchini slices over the potatoes in an even layer.
4. Put ½ tbsp of cream, 2 tbsp of cheese, salt, pepper and oregano over the zucchini.
5. Arrange the tomato slices over the zucchini in an even layer.
6. Put the remaining cream, cheese, salt, pepper and oregano over the tomatoes.
7. Bake in a pre-heated oven at 200°C (400°F) for 20 minutes or till the cheese melts and turns light brown in colour.
8. Remove, divide into 4 equal portions and serve immediately with tomato ketchup.

# Almond Til Chikki

Crunchy munchy chikkis! Who can say no to them, or stop with just one for that matter! These healthy chikkis will not only make your children happy but also meet their calcium requirement.

Nutritive values per piece
Protein: 1.9 gm
Calcium: 62.5 mg

Preparation Time: 10 minutes.    Cooking Time: 10 minutes.    Makes 10 pieces.

¼ cup black sesame seeds (*til*)
½ cup powdered almonds (*badam*)
⅓ cup grated jaggery (*gur*)
1 tsp ghee
½ tsp ghee for greasing

1. Heat a non-stick pan, add the sesame seeds and almonds and roast over a slow flame till they turn light golden in colour. Remove and keep aside to cool.
2. Heat the ghee in the same pan, add the jaggery and simmer over a slow flame while stirring continuously, till the jaggery melts and caramelizes and forms a hard ball when you add a drop in a bowlful of cold water. Remove from the flame.
3. Add the roasted sesame seeds and almonds and mix thoroughly.
4. When slightly cool, divide the mixture into 10 equal pieces and shape each portion into rounds or mould into desire shapes, using different moulds or cookie cutters as shown in the picture.
5. Cool completely and store in an air-tight container.

# Apricot and Walnut Pancakes with Orange Sauce

Sweet pancakes served with warm, tangy orange sauce is nothing short of a treat! And healthy too... for the nuts provide protein and calcium required for the formation of new bone cells and for the growth and maintenance of bones.

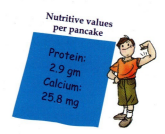

Nutritive values per pancake
Protein: 2.9 gm
Calcium: 25.8 mg

Preparation Time: 10 minutes.   Cooking Time: 25 minutes.   Makes 6 pancakes.

**For the pancake**
½ cup whole wheat flour (*gehun ka atta*)
¾ cup unsweetened soya milk
2 tbsp powdered sugar
Salt to taste
2 tsp fruit salt
1 tbsp oil for cooking

**To be mixed into a stuffing**
1 cup peeled and chopped orange
¼ cup chopped dried apricots (*kuumani / jardalu*)
¼ cup chopped walnuts (*akhrot*)

**For the orange sauce**
¼ cup orange or strawberry marmalade/ jam
1 to 2 drops of lemon juice

**For the pancake**
1. Combine the wheat flour, soyamilk, sugar, salt and fruit salt in a bowl and mix well to make a thick batter.
2. Heat a non-stick pan, pour a laddleful of the batter to make a circle of 100 mm (4") in diameter.
3. Cook on both sides using little oil till it turn golden brown in colour.
4. Repeat with the remaining batter to make 5 more pancakes and keep aside.

**For the orange sauce**
1. Heat a non-stick pan, add the marmalade, lemon juice and ¼ cup water and mix well.
2. Melt it over a low flame and keep aside.

**How to proceed**
1. Divide the stuffing into 6 equal portions and keep aside.
2. Just before serving, arrange a pancake on a serving dish.
3. Place a portion of stuffing over it and spread it evenly. Pour 1 tsp of warm orange sauce over the stuffing.
4. Repeat with the remaining pancakes, stuffing and sauce to make 5 more pancakes and serve immediately.
5. Alternatively make layers of pancakes and stuffing as shown in the picture.

# Burger

Health and taste in one package! Don't eliminate burgers as unhealthy... give this healthy version a chance. Made using whole wheat burger buns and tikkis made with broken wheat, these provide loads of protein and calcium.

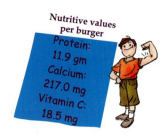

Nutritive values per burger
Protein: 11.9 gm
Calcium: 217.0 mg
Vitamin C: 18.5 mg

**Preparation Time: 25 minutes.    Cooking Time: 25 minutes.    Makes 6 burgers.**

### For the *tikkis*
1/3 cup cooked broken wheat (*dalia*)
2 tbsp finely chopped carrots
2 tbsp finely chopped French beans
2 tbsp cooked sweet corn kernels (*makai ke dane*)
2 medium potatoes, boiled and mashed
1 slice of whole wheat bread
½ tsp finely chopped green chillies
¼ tsp freshly ground pepper
1 tbsp chopped coriander (*dhania*)
1 tbsp oil for cooking
Salt to taste

### Other ingredients
6 whole wheat burger buns
2 tbsp tomato ketchup
12 lettuce leaves
2 medium sized onions, sliced
2 green cucumbers, sliced
2 tomatoes, sliced
Salt to taste
6 slices cheese

### For the *tikkis*
1. Combine all the ingredients together in a bowl and mix well.
2. Divide the mixture into 6 equal portions and shape each portion into an even sized round and flatten the rounds to make *tikkis*.
3. Heat a non-stick pan and cook each *tikki* using ½ tsp oil until both sides are golden brown in colour. Keep aside.

### How to serve
1. Cut each burger bun horizontally into two and toast them lightly in an oven or on a *tava* (griddle).
2. On the lower half of each bun spread 1 tsp of the tomato ketchup and place 2 lettuce leaves over it.
3. Place a few onion slices, cucumber slices, tomato slices and sprinkle a little salt over it.
4. Finally place 1 slice of cheese and 1 *tikki* cover with the remaining half of the bun and press it lightly.
5. Repeat with the remaining ingredients to make 5 more burgers.

### More Burgers
Burgers are a kiddie favourite. They are easy to assemble too!

*Some other options to make a burger instead of the broken wheat tikki are*

Baked beans        Sprouts *subzi*
Potato *tikki*        Soya *tikkis*

# Rajma Spinach and Cheese Triangles

An innovative method of serving otherwise boring rajma and spinach to kids! A combination of calcium-rich ingredients makes these parathas a must-try. Cheese adds a unique flavour and makes it a kids-friendly recipe.

Nutritive values per trangle
Protein: 8.0 gm
Calcium: 130.3 mg
Vitamin C: 20.1 mg

Preparation Time: 15 minutes.    Cooking Time: 25 minutes.    Makes 4 triangles.
Soaking Time: Overnight

**For the dough**
¾ cup whole wheat flour (*gehun ka atta*)
Salt to taste
¼ tsp oil for kneading

**For the *rajma* and spinach mixture**
¼ cup *rajma* (kidney beans), soaked overnight
Salt to taste
2 tsp oil
2 tsp finely chopped garlic
¼ cup finely chopped onions
½ cup finely chopped tomatoes
2 tbsp finely chopped capsicum
½ tsp chilli powder
1 tsp roasted cumin seeds (*jeera*) powder
⅓ cup finely chopped spinach (*palak*)

**Other ingredients**
Whole wheat flour (*gehun ka atta*) for rolling
4 tbsp grated mozzarella cheese
4 tsp oil for cooking

**For the dough**
1. Combine the wheat flour and salt in a bowl and knead into a soft dough using enough water. Keep aside covered with a wet muslin cloth for 10 minutes.
2. Knead again using oil and divide the dough into 4 equal portions and keep aside under a wet muslin cloth.

**For the *rajma* and spinach mixture**
1. Combine the *rajma*, salt and ¾ cup water and pressure cook for 4 to 5 whistles or till the *rajma* turn soft and are slightly overcooked.
2. Drain the *rajma* and grind in a mixer to a coarse paste. Keep aside
3. Heat the oil in a non-stick pan, add the garlic and onions and sauté till the onions turn translucent.
4. Add the tomatoes and sauté for another 3 to 4 minutes.
5. Add the *rajma* mixture, capsicum, chilli powder, cumin seeds powder and salt and mix well.
6. Add the spinach and cook for another 5 minutes or till the mixture becomes dry.
7. Divide the mixture into 4 equal portions and keep aside.

**How to proceed**
1. Roll out each portion of the dough into a 150 mm. (6") diameter circle with using a little flour.
2. Spread a portion of the prepared mixture in the centre and sprinkle 1 tbsp of cheese over it and fold to make a triangle as shown in the picture.
3. Heat a non-stick pan and cook each triangle using 1 tsp of oil till both sides are golden brown in colour.
4. Repeat with the remaining dough and mixture to make 3 more triangles. Serve hot.

# Stir-fried Vegetable Noodles

Stronger bones need more calcium and protein. No worries... here's a colourful and nutrient-rich recipe brimming with the goodness of veggies, sprouts and paneer. Your kids will go gaga over this interesting looking and tangy tasting dish!

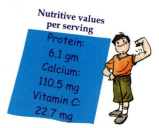

Nutritive values per serving
Protein: 6.1 gm
Calcium: 110.5 mg
Vitamin C: 22.7 mg

Preparation Time: 15 minutes.   Cooking Time: 20 minutes.   Serves 4.

**For the rice noodles**
1 packet rice noodles
1 tsp oil
Salt to taste

**For the sweet and sour sauce (makes approximately ½ cup)**
1 large tomato
2 tsp vinegar
¼ tsp soya sauce
½ tsp chilli sauce
1 tsp sugar
½ tsp cornflour
Salt to taste

**Other ingredients**
1 tbsp olive oil or any other oil
½ cup sliced coloured capsicum (yellow, red and green)
½ cup sliced baby corn, blanched
½ cup *paneer* (cottage cheese) cubes
½ cup chopped pineapple
¼ cup bean sprouts
1 tsp finely chopped celery
Salt to taste

**For the rice noodles**
1. Boil 6 cups of water in a vessel.
2. Remove from flame, add the rice noodles, cover with a lid and keep aside for 10-15 minutes.
3. Drain the water and again dip into cold water in order to arrest any further cooking.
4. Drain again and keep aside.

**For the sweet and sour sauce**
1. Boil a vesselful of water, add the tomatoes and cook for 3-4 minutes. Remove from the flame and keep aside to cool.
2. Remove the skin of the tomatoes and blend in a mixer to a smooth purée.
3. Heat a non-stick pan, add the tomato purée and all the remaining ingredients and mix well.
4. Cook on a medium flame for 8 to 10 minutes or till it becomes thick while stirring continuously. Keep aside.

**How to proceed**
1. Heat the oil in a non-stick pan, add the capsicum, baby corn, *paneer*, pineapple and bean sprouts and sauté on a high flame for a few seconds while stirring continuously.
2. Add the celery and salt, mix well and cook for another minute.
3. Add the prepared sweet and sour sauce, toss well and cook for a few seconds. Serve immediately on the bed of rice noodles.

# Fruity Youghurt

Curds become even more enticing when served with crunchy fruits and cornflakes! For an added visual appeal, chop the fruits in innovative shapes and sizes or use a cookie cutter. Better still... why not get the kids to help you carve the fruits?

Nutritive values per serving
Protein: 4.8 gm
Calcium: 214.9 mg
Vitamin C 1.9 mg

**Preparation Time: 10 minutes.   Cooking Time: Nil.   Serves 4.**

2 cups chopped mixed fruits (watermelon, grapes, papaya, oranges, apples, banana etc)
¾ cup corn flakes/wheat flakes/coco pops etc.

**To be blended together**
2 cups thick fresh curds (*dahi*)
3-4 tbsp powdered sugar
½ tsp vanilla essence (optional)

1. Take a serving glass, pour ¼ cup of the blended curds at the bottom, add ½ cup of fruits and again ¼ cup of the curds over it.
2. Refrigerate to chill.
3. Just before serving top it with corn flakes and serve immediately.

### Chef's Tip!
- Fruits are seasonal and hence best consumed when in season. If you do not find all fruits, use just one variety of fruit for this recipe.
- Fruits and curds may even be blended together and frozen to make fruit candies.
- Fruits are rich in many vitamins and minerals and fibre and this is the least way to make your fussy kids to get their share of nutrients.

# No More Colds

The key to a healthy child is a healthy immune system, which is the body's defence against infection. As children grow they become more adventurous and play in dirt and dust most of the time, eat with dirty hands and are surrounded by infection in the school or while playing making them highly susceptible to such infections.

## How should I boost my child's immunity?

In order to develop and thrive, your child's immune system needs to be nourished with essential nutrients like vitamins C and E, Vitamin A, zinc and selenium, which are required for it to function efficiently. Immune boosters (nutrients and foods) work in many different ways viz. they help to increase the number of white blood cells (soldiers of our body), improve their functioning and enhance their action against infections. Given below is a list of immune-boosting nutrients, their specific functions within the immune system and their sources.

## Vitamin C

Vitamin C is a water-soluble vitamin and is found abundantly in citrus fruits like oranges, sweetlime, pineapple, guava and *amla*, and vegetables like capsicum, cabbage, broccoli, sprouts etc. Include these foods in your child's diet to recharge the immune system. Vitamin C tops the list of immune boosters for many reasons:

▶ Vitamin C is a natural and powerful antioxidant that fights free radicals
▶ Its consumption during the younger years reduces the risk of developing life-threatening illnesses like heart disease, diabetes and cancer later in life.
▶ It nourishes and improves the health of skin, which is our body's first line of defence.

Try and avoid heating or over-cooking foods with vitamin C as the vitamin gets destroyed when exposed to heat. Hence whip up some salads or juices or eat fresh vegetables and fruits.

## Vitamin E

This important antioxidant and immune booster doesn't get as much attention as vitamin C, yet it is important for a healthy immune system. Unlike vitamin C, it is a fat-soluble vitamin and can be stored in the body. The best sources of vitamin E are vegetable oils, including sunflower, safflower, canola, corn, olive, and wheat germ oil; and products made from these oils, such as margarine. Unprocessed cereal grains, broccoli, avocado, oatmeal, flaxseeds, almonds, walnuts, sweet potatoes and leafy-green vegetables also contain vitamin E, but in smaller amounts. It works synergistically with selenium to fight infections and boosts the immune system.

## Vitamin A

Vitamin A has anti-carcinogenic properties and immune-boosting functions as follows.

➤ It increases the number of infection-fighting cells, natural killer cells, and helper T-cells
➤ It is a powerful antioxidant that mops up excess free radicals.

You will find vitamin A in all brightly coloured yellow-red fruits and vegetables like carrots, oranges, apples, melons, mangoes, black grapes, strawberries, plums, broccoli, green leafy vegetables like spinach, fenugreek, colocasia etc.

## Zinc

➤ This valuable mineral increases the production of white blood cells that fight infection and helps them fight more aggressively.
➤ Helps in growth and regeneration of white cells called fighter cells.

Add zinc to your child's diet by including cereals, beans, and fortified cereals.

## *In this section...*

Being well-versed in the varied nature of the above-mentioned nutrients I have chosen ingredients very selectively and avoided cooking them. I have used more of fruits like pineapple, black grapes and oranges, and vegetables like broccoli, cabbage, lettuce, capsicum and bean sprouts etc. Give abundant vitamin C and beta-carotene to your little ones by whipping up simple recipes like **Pasta Salad,** *page 48,* **Pineapple Stir-fry,** *page 52* and **Fruity Sanedsh,** *page 60.*

These recipes call for fresh fruits and veggies and do not involve any cooking, thereby retaining vitamin C. But I have added oil to the salads to enhance the absorption of vitamin A and vitamin E.

Kids love to eat junk foods like pizzas, rolls and sandwiches, so here I present nutritious and healthier versions of such foods made using vital ingredients like mixed vegetables, lettuce, walnuts, corn, spinach, broccoli etc that are sure to keep the kids away from colds. Turn to **Veggie-Mayo Rolls,** *page 46,* **Cheesy Corn and Spinach Pizza,** *page 50,* **Cheese and Broccoli Tikkis,** *page 56* and **Lettuce Spoons,** *page 58.* **Walnut Fudge Fingers,** *page 59* uses walnuts innovatively to satisfy your child's sweet tooth in a healthy way by providing vitamin E and zinc. Besides these fingers serve **Sunshine Boost,** *page 48* and **Fruit Lollies,** *page 54* to quench thirst instead of artificial fruit drinks that are laden with calories and preservatives.

Add these delicious recipes to your child's diet to cut down on the days missed from school because of illness.

# Veggie-Mayo Rolls

If you remember the popular British Airways ad, "Kids walk to school and run back home." And well, probably in anticipation of the snacks you'd have laid out on the table! Treat them to these tasty and healthy whole wheat bread rolls stuffed with a combination of veggies and mayonnaise.

**Nutritive values per roll**
Vitamin C: 1.0 mg
Vitamin A: 151.7 mcg

Preparation Time: 10 minutes.   Cooking Time: 10 minutes.   Makes 8 rolls.
Baking Temperature: 200°C (400°F).   Baking Time: 20 minutes.

4 hot dog rolls (brown bread), 6" long
1 tsp butter

**To be mixed into a topping**
½ cup chopped and boiled mixed vegetables (French beans, carrots, green peas, potatoes, cauliflower etc.)
½ cup shredded lettuce
¼ cup cooked sweet corn kernels (*makai ke dane*)
2 tbsp finely chopped celery
1½ tbsp finely chopped walnuts (*akhrot*)

½ cup mayonnaise
Salt and freshly ground pepper to taste

**How to proceed**
1. Cut each roll into 2 halves horizontally.
2. Butter each half lightly and toast on a non-stick *tava* (griddle) for about 5 minutes. Keep aside.
3. Divide the topping into 8 equal portions.
4. Spread one portion of the topping evenly on one half of the roll.
5. Repeat with the remaining ingredients to make 7 more rolls. Serve immediately.

## Yummy toppings

*Given below are French breads, find out the topping on each by reading the letters written on it. The trick is to know which letter comes first, start reading to the right, or to the left.*

46

# Pasta Salad

Nutritive values per serving
Vitamin A: 196.7 mcg
Vitamin C: 19.4 mg
Vitamin E: 1.6 mg

Your kids can say goodbye to colds and other infections with this immune-boosting salad made with an interesting combination of vitamins A, C and E rich ingredients.

Preparation Time: 15 minutes.   Cooking Time: Nil.   Serves 4.

½ cup boiled pasta
¼ cup blanched broccoli florets
¼ cup chopped pineapple
¼ cup chopped black grapes
2 tbsp finely shredded cabbage
2 tbsp cooked sweet corn kernels (*makai ke dane*)
2 tbsp thickly grated carrots
2 tbsp chopped almonds (*badam*)

**To be mixed into a dressing**
2 tbsp pineapple purée
Salt and freshly ground pepper to taste

1. Combine all the ingredients in a bowl and mix well. Refrigerate to chill.
2. Just before serving pour the dressing and toss well.
   Serve immediately.

# Sunshine Boost

Nutritive values per glass
Vitamin C: 95.0 mg
Vitamin A: 2183.4 mcg

Fruits and veggies boost one's immunity as they are rich in natural antioxidants, vitamins A and C. Cooking destroys these vitamins, and so it is better to have them raw as in this recipe.

Preparation Time: 10 minutes.   Cooking Time: Nil.   Makes 4 glasses.

4 medium sized carrots (unpeeled), cut into pieces
2 medium sized oranges (peeled), separated into segments
2 *amla* (Indian gooseberry), deseeded and cut into pieces
2 tbsp powdered sugar
Crushed ice for serving

1. Combine all the ingredients except the ice in a mixer and blend till smooth.
2. Strain the juice using a strainer or a muslin cloth.
3. Add some crushed ice into 4 individual glasses and pour the juice over it.
   Serve immediately.

# Cheesy Corn and Spinach Pizza

Who would have thought that pizzas, which are normally categorised as junk food, can be easily transformed into a healthy dish by using corn and spinach rotis instead of the unhealthy pizza base that is made with refined flour (maida)! Also, cheese and corn help perk up the flavour along with pizza sauce. Wheat germ enhances immunity as it is rich in vitamin E, a natural antioxidant that fights disease-causing germs.

Nutritive values per pizza
Vitamin C: 13.2 mg
Vitamin E: 0.5 mg
Vitamin A: 370.0 mcg

Preparation Time: 15 minutes.   Cooking Time: 20 minutes.   Makes 7 mini pizzas.
Baking Temperature: 150°C (300°F).   Baking Time: 20 minutes.

### For the corn and spinach *rotis*
½ cup whole wheat flour (*gehun ka atta*)
¼ cup cooked sweet corn kernels (*makai ke dane*), crushed
¼ cup finely chopped spinach (*palak*)
2 tbsp wheat germ
Salt to taste

### For the pizza sauce
4 medium sized tomatoes
2 tsp butter
¼ cup chopped onions
2 tsp chopped garlic
1 tsp oregano
1 tsp sugar
Salt to taste

### Other ingredients
½ cup grated mozzarella cheese

### For the corn and spinach *rotis*
1. Combine all the ingredients together in a bowl and knead into a soft dough using water as required. Keep aside covered with a wet muslin cloth.
2. Knead again and divide the dough into 7 equal portions and roll out each portion into 75 mm (3") diameter *roti*. Alternatively cut into desired shapes using different cookie cutters as shown in the picture.
3. Heat a non-stick pan and cook each *roti* lightly till brown spots appear on both the sides. Keep aside.

### For the pizza sauce
1. Boil a vesselful of water, add the tomatoes and simmer for 10 minutes.
2. Remove the skin and blend in a mixer to a smooth purée. Keep aside.
3. Heat the butter in a non-stick pan, add the onions and garlic and sauté for at least 5 minutes.
4. Add the tomato purée, ¼ cup of water, oregano, sugar and salt and simmer for 5 to 7 minutes or till the liquid evaporates.
5. Remove and divide the sauce into 4 equal portions and keep aside.

### How to proceed
1. Place a *roti* on a clean dry surface, spread one portion of the pizza sauce evenly on it and sprinkle 1 tbsp of cheese over it.
2. Bake in a pre-heated oven for 15 minutes or till the *roti* is crisp and the cheese melts.
3. Repeat with remaining ingredients to make 6 more pizzas and serve immediately.

# Pineapple Stir-fry

An unusual and eclectic combination of ingredients makes this dish a chartbuster! Cook this dish minimally to retain most of the vitamin C it has.

**Nutritive values per serving**
Vitamin C: 66.8 mg
Vitamin A: 364.5 mcg

Preparation Time: 15 minutes.    Cooking Time: 6 to 8 minutes.    Serves 4.

2 tbsp oil
1 tsp dry red chilli flakes
½ cup pineapple cubes
½ cup carrot cubes, blanched
½ cup zucchini cubes, blanched
½ cup bean sprouts
½ cup blanched baby corn, cut into 25 mm. (1") pieces
½ cup shredded cabbage
½ red capsicum, cut into cubes
½ cup thinly sliced spring onion whites
Salt to taste
½ cup finely chopped spring onion greens
½ cup fresh pineapple juice

2 tsp soya sauce
1 tsp sugar

1. Heat the oil in a wok on a high flame, add the chilli flakes, pineapple, carrot, zucchini, bean sprouts, baby corn, cabbage, capsicum, spring onion whites and salt and stir-fry on a high flame for 3 to 4 minutes.
2. Add the spring onion greens, pineapple juice, soya sauce and sugar and stir-fry for 3 to 4 more minutes.
Serve immediately.

## "P" Pyramid
*Listed below are a few questions, find the answers and write them in correct order to fill the pyramid.*

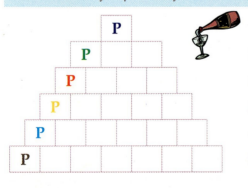

1. A small green vegetable found in a pod ③
2. _____ the water in a glass ④
3. A utensil used to serve food ⑤
4. Salt and _____ to taste ⑥
5. _____ the oven before baking ⑦

**Clue:** All answers start with the letter P and are related to cooking. Browse through the recipes in this book to find them.

# Fruit Lollies

Lollies are all-time favourite... to the extent of being one of the most interesting aspects of childhood! Unlike their commercial counterparts, these fruit lollies don't use artificial flavours and colours. Instead, they provide lots of nutrients including vitamins C and A. Ensure that the fruits are completely ripe and sweet to avoid adding more sugar.

Nutritive values per serving
Vitamin C: 30.1 mg
Vitamin A: 493.2 mcg

Preparation Time: 5 minutes.   Cooking Time: Nil.   Serves 4.

½ cup freshly squeezed pineapple juice
½ cup freshly squeezed orange juice
2 tbsp strawberry pulp mixed in 1½ tsp powdered sugar

1. Add ½ tsp of sugar to all the juices and keep aside.
2. Take small glasses or candy moulds of desired shapes, pour 2 tbsp of pineapple juice at the bottom of each mould and refrigerate to set.
3. When fully set, pour 2 tbsp of orange juice in each glass to make a layer and refrigerate to set without disturbing.
4. When fully set, pour 2 tbsp of strawberry mixture in each glass and refrigerate again to set for atleast an hour.
5. Just before serving, hold the glasses under a running tap and take out the lollies.
Serve immediately.

### Make your favourite lollies with the ideas listed below :

- Banana, roasted oats and oranges, blend together with milk and freeze to make a sweet and tangy lolly.
- Strawberry Banana Lollies.
- Orange Chocolate Lollies.
- Plum and Apple Lollies.
- Chikoo Milk Lollies.
- Pineapple Celery Lollies.

# Cheese and Broccoli Tikkis

Given a choice, kids will say nyaaaaah to broccoli, but they are a must-have because of their nutritional benefits! So, tempt them with these yummy tikkis made with a combination of broccoli and cheese. Use olive oil to cook these tikkis as it is rich in vitamin E.

Nutritive values per *tikki*
Vitamin C: 10.7 mg
Vitamin E: 0.5 mcg
Vitamin A: 319.4 mcg

Preparation Time: 15 minutes.    Cooking Time: 15 minutes.    Makes 4 *tikkis*.

1 tsp olive oil
¼ cup finely chopped onions
1 tsp ginger-garlic paste
1 tsp finely chopped green chillies
½ cup finely chopped broccoli
Salt to taste
½ cup boiled and grated potatoes
2 tbsp grated mozzarella cheese
¼ cup whole wheat bread crumbs for coating
2 tsp olive oil for cooking

1. Heat the oil in a non-stick pan, add the onions, ginger-garlic paste and green chillies and sauté for 2 minutes while stirring continuously.
2. Add the broccoli and salt and sauté on a slow flame for another 5 to 7 minutes or till the broccoli is almost cooked.
3. Remove from the flame, add the potatoes and cheese and mix well. Keep aside to cool.
4. Divide the mixture into 4 equal portions and shape each portion into flat *tikkis*. Alternatively make *tikkis* of desired shapes using different moulds as shown in the picture.
5. Roll each *tikki* in the bread crumbs and keep aside.
6. Heat a non-stick pan and cook each *tikki* using ½ tsp of oil till it turns golden brown on both the sides.
Serve hot.

## Find the missing food

*In each of the shapes is the name of a fruit, one letter from the word is missing! Find out the missing letter to finish the word (name of the fruit) and write it down. All the missing letters spell the name of a food that kids love.*

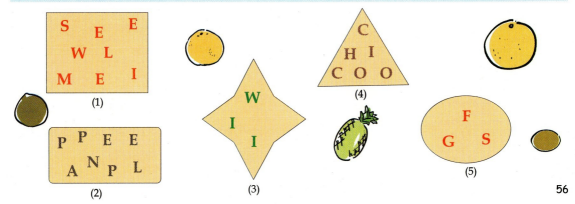

# Lettuce Spoons

Lettuce has a nice crunchy feel which you can exploit to make interesting dishes that please the kids... whether a simple salad or these scrumptious spoons! Lettuce is a good source of vitamins A and C and therefore a great addition to your child's diet. Use tender lettuce leaves and remove any veins before using. Serving in a spoon makes it interesting and nutritious snack that is fine to appeal your little brats.

Nutritive values per serving
Vitamin C: 3.5 mg
Vitamin A: 173.0 mcg

Preparation Time: 10 minutes.   Cooking Time: 5 minutes.   Serves 4 (Makes 16 spoons).

4 to 5 lettuce leaves

**To be mixed into a filling**
1½ tbsp crumbled *paneer* (cottage cheese)
1½ tbsp chopped pineapple
1½ tbsp grated carrots
1½ tbsp finely chopped celery
1½ tbsp finely chopped walnuts (*akhrot*)
1½ tbsp eggless mayonnaise
Salt and freshly ground pepper to taste

1. Wash the lettuce leaves, dry them on a towel and cut each leaf into 50 mm. (2") squares. Immense in ice-cold water for 10 minutes to keep them crisp. Drain and keep aside.
2. Place a lettuce square on a soup spoon and put 2 tsp of the filling in the centre.
3. Repeat with remaining lettuce squares and filling to make 15 more spoons and serve immediately.

# Walnut Fudge Fingers

Walnuts are a storehouse of nutrients! This finger food made using kids' favourites such as biscuits, cocoa powder, sugar, etc., is a smart way of sneaking walnuts into their little tummies. Butter is a rich source of vitamin A, but that does not license you to use it in whopping amounts, as it is also high in fats. So cook smart, and ensure your kids stay healthy!

Nutritive values per finger

Vitamin A: 274.0 mcg

Preparation Time: 10 minutes.   Cooking Time: 10 minutes.   Makes 10 fingers.

½ cup butter
½ cup sugar
2 tbsp milk
2 tbsp cocoa powder
A pinch salt
½ tsp vanilla essence
1 cup powdered digestive biscuits
¼ tsp butter for greasing
4 tbsp finely chopped walnuts (*akhrot*)

1. Heat a non-stick pan, add the butter, sugar, milk, cocoa powder and salt and mix well.
2. Simmer on a slow flame till the sugar melts. Remove from the flame and keep aside for 10 minutes.
3. When the mixture slightly cools, add the vanilla essence and mix well.
4. Add the powdered biscuits and mix thoroughly.
5. Divide the mixture into 20 equal portions and shape each portion into an oblong finger or desired shapes using different moulds as shown in the picture.
6. Roll each finger in the walnuts and refrigerate to chill.
Serve immediately.

# Fruity Sandesh

Put together a super duper dessert with fruits and paneer, delighting your kids' palates while at the same time helping them stock up on vitamins A and C. These chilled sandesh will be a welcome refreshment when your child comes home exhausted after a day at school!

Nutritive values per serving
Vitamin A: 602.2 mcg
Vitamin C: 18.7 mg

Preparation Time: 15 minutes.    Cooking Time: 10 minutes.    Serves 4.

**For the orange sauce**
¼ cup freshly squeezed orange juice
¼ tsp cornflour mixed with 2 tsp water
1½ tsp honey

**To be blended together into orange sandesh**
¼ cup freshly made *paneer* (cottage cheese)
2 tsp powdered sugar
¾ tsp flavoured orange drink mix

**Other ingredients**
4 orange segments for the topping
1 small banana cut into thick roundles for the topping

**For the orange sauce**
1. Heat a non-stick pan, add the orange juice and cornflour paste and mix well.
2. Simmer on a slow flame while stirring continuously till it thickens.
3. Add the honey, mix well and simmer for another 1 minute.
4. Remove form the flame and keep aside.

**How to proceed**
1. Divide the orange sandesh into 4 equal portions and keep aside.
2. Take each orange segment, slit vertically along the centre of the broad side and open it to make a round. Keep aside.
3. Take a small glass plate, put one portion of the orange sanesh at the bottom and spread it evenly.
4. Arrange an orange segment and bananas evenly over it. Refrigerate to chill.
5. Warm the orange sauce and keep aside.
6. Just before serving, pour 1 tbsp of the warm orange sauce over the fruits and serve immediately.
7. Repeat with the remaining ingredients to make 3 more servings.

Here are some more variations of Sandesh served with yummy sauces
- Mango Sandesh topped with chopped mangoes and mango sauce.
- Dry fruit sandesh with butterscotch sauce.
- Mixed fruit sandesh with chocolate sauce.
- Banana sandesh with strawberry sauce.

# Fibre Rich Recipes

## What is fibre and why does my child need it?

Fibre is an important part of a healthy diet for your child. Fibre, also known as "roughage", is found in the cell walls of plants and is made up of a number of complex carbohydrates that cannot be digested by the body. It is an essential nutrient as it aids the process of digestion, and the lack of it in your child's diet can result in irregular bowel movements and constipation. This may further affect the absorption of nutrients, accumulation of wastes and toxins in the body and various other health problems. Dietary fibre has important health benefits for your child now and for his or her entire lifetime.

## Types of fibre

Fibre can be classified as insoluble or soluble:

1. **Insoluble fibre** is not soluble in water and increases the bulk of the intestinal contents. Wheat, other cereals, and wheat bran are good sources of insoluble fibre. Role of this fibre in digestion is as follows:

   ▶ It has the ability to speed up the rate at which food moves along the intestine.

   ▶ It promotes regularity in bowel movements and helps alleviate constipation.

   ▶ It binds to harmful substances and eliminates them quickly through the digestive system.

2. **Soluble fibre** is soluble in water and has the ability to absorb water like a sponge, swelling, and therefore increasing the bulk of the intestinal contents. It can be found in foods such as apples (with the skin), pears, prunes, oats, barley, green peas, sprouts and other fruits.

   ▶ Soluble fibre lowers blood sugar levels and reduces cholesterol from the blood thereby lowering the risk of developing degenerative disorders like diabetes, heart attacks etc. at a later age.

Along with fibre, water is another important nutrient. Your child's body contains a lot of fluid. In fact, 50-70% of the human body is made up of fluid, and in children, it's closer to the 70% mark. Water is very important for the following reasons:

- Water in the blood is the chief vehicle for the distribution of essential nutrients and oxygen throughout the body.
- Water also helps your child swallow and digest foods.
- It hydrates the child's body, aids fibre in the process of digestion and keeps your child's body temperature normal.

Water can be provided in the form of plain water, milk, fruit juices and milk shakes. Anything that increases water loss from the body, such as strenuous exercise, hot weather, diarrhoea or fever, increases the body's need for water. Your child should drink at least 5 glasses of water daily.

## *In this section...*

I have included recipes like **Toasted Stuffed Chapatis**, *page 68* and **Cheese Chilli Frisbees**, *page 72*, made from whole wheat flour that is full of fibre. Green peas, brimming with fibre are made into delicious **Green Peas and Paneer Mini Parathas**, *page 64* and **Green Pea and Corn Bhel**, *page 74*. Fruits like apples, pineapple, papaya etc. can be included in a child's diet in the form of **Papaya Pineapple Juice**, *page 64*, **Oats Pineapple Sheera**, *page 70* and **Apple and Cheese Toasts**, *page 72*.

Macaroni, though made from *maida* is most popular with kids, and so, to please their palates I used have them. However, I have added fibre by adding lots of vegetables. Refer to **Merry Macaroni**, *page 66*.

Similarly a veggie boost is added to make recipes fibre-rich, as in **Kashmiri Fresh Fruit Rice**, *page 67* and **Mini Mixed Vegetable Turnovers**, *page 70*.

# Green Peas and Paneer Mini Parathas

Fibre is much-needed at any age, but it could be tough getting your kids to consume fibre-rich food, unless served in a form as interesting as these luscious parathas!

Nutritive values per *paratha*
Fibre: 0.5 gm

Preparation Time: 10 minutes.  Cooking Time: 20 minutes.  Makes 10 mini *parathas*.

½ cup whole wheat flour (*gehun ka atta*)
¼ cup soya flour
½ cup fresh green peas, boiled and roughly crushed
¼ cup grated *paneer* (cottage cheese)
1½ tsp finely chopped green chillies
2 tbsp chopped coriander (*dhania*)
Salt to taste
¼ tsp oil for kneading
5 tsp ghee for cooking

1. Combine all the ingredients together in a bowl and knead into a soft dough.
2. Knead again using oil and keep aside under a wet muslin cloth for 10 minutes.
3. Divide the dough into 10 equal portions and roll out each portion into a thick circle of 75 mm (3") in diameter.
4. Heat a non-stick pan and cook each *paratha* using ½ tsp ghee till both sides are golden brown in colour. Serve hot.

# Papaya Pineapple Juice

Surprise your kid with this unusual combination of papaya and pineapple! Let the little one explore the tangy taste even while topping up on varied nutrients and fibre! A glass of this juice provides 1.5 gm of fibre, which aids in digestion.

Nutritive values per glass
Fibre: 1.5 gm

Preparation Time: 10 minutes.  Cooking Time: Nil.  Makes 2 glasses.

2 cups papaya cubes
1 cup pineapple cubes
¼ cup crushed ice-cubes for serving

1. Combine all the ingredients together in a mixer and blend along with little water (if required) till smooth.
2. Place ice-cubes into 2 individual glasses, pour the juice over it and serve immediately.

# Merry Macaroni

Truly merry as the name suggests! Loaded with the goodness of vegetables and embellished with the looks and texture of macaroni that kids usually love, your children will empty their plates before you can spell m-a-c-a-r-o-n-i!

Nutritive values per serving
Fibre: 1.2 gm

Preparation Time: 10 minutes.    Cooking Time: 10 minutes.    Serves 4.

2 tsp butter
¼ cup finely chopped onions
2 tbsp chopped carrots, blanched
2 tbsp boiled fresh green peas
2 tbsp chopped capsicum
½ cup tomato purée
¼ tsp chilli powder
½ tsp sugar
2 cups boiled macaroni
Salt to taste

1. Heat the butter in a non-stick pan, add the onions and sauté for 1 minute.
2. Add the carrots, green peas and capsicum and sauté for 2 minutes.
3. Add the tomato purée, chilli powder, sugar and 1 tbsp of water. Mix well and simmer for another 3 to 4 minutes.
4. Add the macaroni and salt, mix gently and cook for few seconds. Serve hot.

# Kashmiri Fresh Fruit Rice

A rich, creamy rice dish made more interesting thanks to a delicious mixture of fresh fruits and dry fruits. Condiments like cloves, cinnamon and cardamom impart their unique flavours and make this an irresistible delicacy, especially with kids.

**Nutritive values per serving**
Fibre: 1.0 gm

Preparation Time: 20 minutes.  Cooking Time: 30 minutes.  Serves 4.

1 tbsp ghee
3 cloves *(laung / lavang)*
25 mm. (1") piece cinnamon *(dalchini)*
3 green cardamom *(elaichi)*
1 bayleaf *(tejpatta)*
1 cup mixed fresh fruit cubes (pineapple, oranges, pears, apples, guavas, etc.)
2 cups cooked long grained rice *(basmati)*
2 tbsp chopped mixed nuts (walnuts, cashewnuts, almonds, raisins, etc.)
2 tbsp rose water
1 tsp sugar
1 tbsp fresh cream
¼ cup milk
Salt to taste

1. Heat the ghee in a pan, add the cloves, cinnamon, cardamom and bayleaf and sauté for a few seconds.
2. Add the mixed fruits and sauté for another minute.
3. Add the rice, mixed nuts, rose water, sugar, cream, milk and salt. Mix well and cook for 4 to 5 minutes.
   Serve immediately.

# Toasted Stuffed Chapatis

Give the everyday chapati a kid-friendly makeover! Prepare these chapatis in advance and toast them just before serving to put together a snack that kids will love. Cut each chapati into small pieces, so it fits easily into the eager little mouths!

Nutritive values per serving
Fibre: 0.5 gm

Preparation Time: 10 minutes.   Cooking Time: 20 minutes.   Serves 4.

**For the stuffing**
1 tsp oil
2 tbsp chopped spring onions (with greens)
2 tbsp sprouted *moong* (whole green gram), boiled
2 tbsp grated boiled potatoes
2 tbsp grated *paneer* (cottage cheese)
2 tbsp chopped coriander (*dhania*)
1 tsp chilli powder
Salt to taste

**Other ingredients**
4 leftover whole wheat *chapatis*
2 tbsp grated mozzarella cheese
¼ tsp oil for greasing
2 tsp oil for cooking

**For the stuffing**
1. Heat the oil in a non-stick pan, add the onions and sauté for 2 minutes.
2. Add the *moong*, potatoes, *paneer*, coriander, chilli powder and salt. Mix well and cook for another 5 minutes.
3. Divide the stuffing into 2 equal portions and keep aside.

**How to proceed**
1. Place a *chapati* on a flat dry surface, spread one portion of the stuffing evenly on the chapati and sprinkle 1 tbsp of cheese over it.
2. Cover with another *chapati* and press it lightly.
3. Heat a non-stick pan and grease it lightly with oil. Cook the stuffed *chapatis* using 1 tsp of oil till brown spots appear on both the sides.
4. Repeat with the remaining *chapatis* and stuffing to make 1 more stuffed *chapati*.
5. Cut each stuffed *chapati* into half and serve hot.

# Mini Mixed Vegetable Turnovers

Just buy readymade dosa batter, add the veggies and quickly whip up some delectable turnovers for your little ones. Peanuts and sesame seeds add nutrients as well as crunch to these turnovers.

Nutritive values per serving
Fibre: 0.5 gm

Preparation Time: 10 minutes.   Cooking Time: 20 minutes.   Makes 8 turnovers.

1 cup readymade *dosa* batter
½ cup grated mixed vegetables (carrots, cabbage, cauliflower, onions etc.)
1½ tbsp powdered roasted peanuts
2 tbsp chopped coriander (*dhania*)
1 tsp sugar
1 tsp chilli powder
Salt to taste
2 tsp sesame seeds (*til*) for the topping
2 tsp oil for cooking
8 tsp tomato ketchup for serving

1. Combine together the *dosa* batter, vegetables, peanuts, coriander, sugar, chilli powder, salt and 2 tbsp water in a bowl and mix well. Keep aside.
2. Heat a non-stick pan and grease it lightly with oil.
3. Sprinkle ½ tsp of sesame seeds on it.
4. When they crackle, pour a ladleful of the batter and spread it evenly to make a circle of 75 mm (3") diameter.
5. Cook using ½ tsp of oil, till both sides are golden brown in colour.
6. Repeat with the remaining batter to make 7 more turnovers.
Serve hot with tomato ketchup.

# Oats Pineapple Sheera

Pineapple purée imparts sweetness and a fruity flavour to this sheera. Nutritious and highly recommended for kids, serve warm sheera early in the morning or chill it to serve as a dessert, whichever way your child relishes it the most.

Nutritive values per serving
Fibre: 1.0 gm

Preparation Time: 10 minutes.   Cooking Time: 20 minutes.   Serves 4.

1 tbsp ghee
1 cup quick cooking rolled oats
½ cup pineapple purée
½ cup sugar
1 cup milk
1 tbsp sliced almonds (*badam*) for the garnish

1. Heat the ghee in a non-stick pan, add the oats and sauté till they turn light brown in colour while stirring continuously.
2. Add the pineapple purée and sauté for 5 to 7 minutes while stirring continuously.
3. Add the sugar, milk and ½ cup of water and simmer for 10 minutes or till the liquid evaporates.
Serve hot garnished with almonds.

# Cheese Chilli Frisbees

These mini frisbees are easy-to-make and utterly delicious! You can make these in advance and store in an air-tight container for days. These frisbees can be packed to school, have as it is or topped with sauce and vegetables to make a wholesome and filling snack.

Nutritive values per frisbee
Fibre: 0.8 gm

Preparation Time: 15 minutes.   Cooking Time: 20 minutes.   Makes 6 frisbees.

½ cup whole wheat flour (*gehun ka atta*)
2½ tbsp grated cooking cheese
¼ tsp chili powder
1 tsp sesame seeds (*til*), black and white
2 tbsp wheat bran (*konda*)
1 tsp oil
Salt to taste

1. Combine all the ingredients together in a bowl and knead into a firm dough using enough water.
2. Keep aside for 10 minutes under a wet muslin cloth.
3. Knead again and divide the dough into 6 equal portions.
4. Roll out each portion into thick circles of 100 mm. (4") in diameter.
5. Heat a non-stick pan and cook each circle over a low flame pressing on both the sides with a cloth till they turn light brown and crisp.
6. Cool and store in an air-tight container.

# Apple and Cheese Toasts

These toasts are sure to delight your little ones' taste buds and gift them a bounty of nutrients! For an interesting twist, cut the toasts diagonally to form triangles just before serving.

Nutritive values per toast
Fibre: 0.5 gm

Preparation Time: 5 minutes.   Cooking Time: Nil.   Makes 4 toasts.
Baking Temperature: 200°C (400°F).   Baking Time: 10 to 12 minutes.

2 tsp butter
4 whole wheat bread slices
½ cup grated apples
4 tbsp grated mozzarella cheese for the topping
2 tbsp grated carrots for the topping

1. Apply ½ tsp butter on each bread slice and keep aside.
2. Place the bread slices, with the buttered sides facing upwards, on a clean flat surface and spread 2 tbsp of apples evenly on each slices.
3. Sprinkle 1 tbsp of cheese and 1½ tsp of carrots over each slice and bake them in a pre-heated oven at 200°C (400°F) for 5 to 7 minutes or till the cheese melts. Serve hot.

# Green Pea and Corn Bhel

Two of my favourite ingredients join hands here to make a fibre-rich feast for my little buddies! This is indeed a healthy choice of chaat as it is full of healthy ingredients like green peas, vegetables and corn, flavoured with khatti-meethi chutney.

Nutritive values per serving
Fibre: 3.0 gm

Preparation Time: 10 minutes.    Cooking Time: 10 minutes.    Serves 4.

2 tsp oil
1 tsp cumin seeds (*jeera*)
¼ cup chopped onions
1 cup boiled green peas
1 cup cooked sweet corn kernels (*makai ke dane*)
¼ cup chopped boiled potatoes
2 tbsp chopped tomatoes
Salt to taste
¼ cup *khatti-meethi chutney*, page 26
½ tsp *chaat masala*
1 tbsp finely chopped coriander (*dhania*)
2 tbsp *sev* and 2 tbsp pomegranate seeds (*anardana*) for the garnish

1. Heat the oil in a non-stick pan and add the cumin seeds.
2. When the crackle, add the onions and sauté for 2 minutes.
3. Add the green peas, corn and potatoes and mix well. Remove from the flame and keep aside to cool.
4. When cool, add the tomatoes, salt, *khatti-meethi chutney*, *chaat masala* and coriander and mix well.
   Serve immediately garnished with *sev* and pomegranate seeds.

## Make your own bhel

*Listed below are the names of some ingredients that make a bhel. Pick up an appropriate letter from the box and fill in the blank space to finish the word that spells a food.*

E U T N O T I O

A C D S ☐ V K I J
M P E A ☐ U T S L
Z Q R P ☐ R I I T
T O M A ☐ O E S O
P U F F E D R ☐ C E S T
Y L M N ☐ N I O N S
T L E M ☐ N Z P A
M C H U ☐ N E Y Q

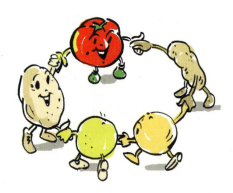

74

# "I Scored the Highest"

The most rapid brain growth occurs during the first year of life, with the infant's brain tripling in size by the first birthday. For your child to be active both at school and at play, and to carry on with day-to-day activities, his brain should work efficiently. To do so it is important that your child eats well, in order to feed the brain cells with required nutrients. Nutrients like carbohydrates, proteins, fats, B-complex vitamins, zinc, iron and calcium enhance the activity of brain cells and help them function well.

**Let us review each brain-boosting nutrient and its role in brain development...**

Brain needs enough energy to perform its functions. Energy is supplied through the food we eat, through the nutrients that provide energy like carbohydrates, protein and fat.

**Carbohydrate** is a fuel for your child's brain. Complex carbohydrates are digested slowly and give a steady supply of energy to the brain compared to simple carbohydrates.

As a mother you must have noticed that your child's behaviour often deteriorates later in the day, or three to four hours after a meal. It is because children simply run out of fuel, and thus it is important to refuel them every 2 to 3 hours. A heavy breakfast early in the morning and healthy snacks in-between meals helps to do so. Let your child nibble, or graze, on nutritious foods throughout the day. Keep a supply of healthy snacks like fruits, fresh fruit juice, whole-wheat cookies, vegetable sandwiches, *khakhras* etc. readily available at home.

**Protein** is another important nutrient required for the formation of brain cells, its growth and maintenance, right from infancy till the brain is fully matured. Including good quality protein foods in your child's diet ensures a well-developed brain and good cognition as discussed in earlier section.

**Fat** is a major component of the brain cell membrane. Oils from plant sources such as olive, soyabeans, peanut oil, and foods like wheat germ, flax seeds, walnuts, olives etc contain beneficial fats that are brain building, in contrast to foods like butter, ghee, margarine etc that are fattening. Try to include oils (though in moderate amounts) in your child's diet right from an early age to foster brain development.

Besides these major nutrients, there are certain vitamins and minerals that also play a key role in brain development and improve learning, cognition etc.

- **Iron** is a crucial nutrient that helps in blood circulation and serves as a carrier of oxygen and other vital nutrients to the brain cells. This is turn aids in increasing your little one's academic performance. So include more of green leafy vegetables, whole grains like ragi, bajra etc. and nuts and oilseeds.

- **Vitamin C** is required by the brain to make neurotransmitters and to repair the wear and tear of the tissues.

- **B-complex vitamins** are very important. We would literally be lost without these. Besides memory, these nutrients feed and regulate the brain and nervous system. B vitamins are an important part of the brain's diet, as can be noted from the below pointers:

    1. **Vitamin $B_1$ (thiamine, vitamin $B_2$ (riboflavin), and vitamin $B_3$ (niacin)** are required for energy production, by regulating the metabolism of carbohydrates, protein and fat, which in turn fuel the brain cells and the body.

    2. **Vitamin $B_{12}$** is vital for maintaining a healthy myelin sheath, the tissue that covers and insulates brain nerves.

    3. **Vitamin $B_6$** deficiency causes a child to be hyperirritable and fatigued.

    4. **Folic acid** is crucial for the growth and maintenance of brain cells and thereby regulates the brain's normal functions. It aids in the production of DNA and RNA, the body's genetic material, and is especially important during periods of high growth such as infancy, adolescence and pregnancy. Its deficiency seems to affect neurotransmitter function, resulting in symptoms associated with depression.

Eating a well balanced diet comprising of all five food groups viz. cereals, pulses, milk and milk products, fruits and vegetables will provide your child all the above-mentioned B complex vitamins.

➤ Calcium is not only important for growing bones, but also for growing brains. Children with calcium deficiency may show impaired behaviour and learning. Hence, give the required amount of calcium to your child.

## *In this section...*

This section comprises of recipes providing a horde of nutrients vital for brain development like carbohydrates, protein, fat, B-complex vitamins, vitamin C, iron and calcium. I have carefully planned recipes using foods rich in complex carbohydrates like whole wheat flour, pulses, broken wheat etc. Turn to recipes like **Mini Raisin Muffins**, *page 82*, **Vegetable Houses**, *page 84* and **Pulse Appe**, *page 90*, and to get a good amount of carbohydrates, protein and B-complex vitamins like $B_1$ and $B_3$, while recipes like **Paneer Papad Kurkure**, *page 92*, provide ample vitamin $B_2$. To get enough folic acid, iron and calcium cook recipes like **Chana Spinach Rice**, *page 79*, **Almond Sheera**, *page 80*, and **Spinach Malfati**, *page 88*, **Labneh with Crispy Vegetables**, *page 94*, provides vitamin C and fibre whereas **Muesli Coated Fruits**, *page 86*, is nutritious and is a veritable storehouse of essential fatty acids, B-complex vitamins, vitamin C, carbohydrates etc.

Hence, encourage your children to eat healthy by including a variety of foods like these in their diet and watch them perform brilliantly!

# Chana Spinach Rice

Chana and spinach will take your kids right to the top of their class' rank list! They are rich in folic acid, protein, calcium and other nutrients that sharpen one's brains. If you have cooked rice at hand, this dish can be put together in a jiffy.

Nutritive values per serving
Protein: 4.1 gm
Calcium: 30.2 mg
Folic Acid: 19.6 mcg

Preparation Time: 20 minutes.    Cooking Time: 10 to 12 minutes.    Serves 4.

2 tsp oil
½ cup sliced onions
1 tsp ginger-garlic paste
½ cup chopped capsicum
½ cup chopped tomatoes
½ cup chopped spinach (*palak*)
¼ tsp turmeric powder (*haldi*)
1 tsp chilli powder
1 tsp coriander-cumin seeds (*dhania-jeera*) powder
Salt to taste
1 cup soaked and boiled red *chana* (whole red gram)
2½ cups cooked long grain rice (*basmati*)

1. Heat the oil in a non-stick pan, add the onions and sauté till they turn light brown in colour.
2. Add the ginger-garlic paste, capsicum and tomatoes and sauté for 2 minutes.
3. Add the spinach, turmeric powder, chilli powder, coriander-cumin seeds powder, salt and 2 tbsp of water and cook for 2 to 3 minutes.
4. Add the *chana* and rice, mix gently and cook for another 5 minutes.
Serve hot.

# Almond Sheera

Almond, an age-old brain food is here to do wonders for your child. It is rich in beneficial fats, protein, iron and vitamin B₂... nutrients that boost brain power. Make it often to keep your kids mentally agile!

Nutritive values per serving
Protein: 13.3 gm
Iron: 2.6 mg
Vitamin B₂: 0.3 mg

Preparation Time: 15 minutes.   Cooking Time: 10 minutes.   Serves 4.

1 cup blanched almonds (*badam*)
¾ cup milk
1 tbsp ghee
½ cup sugar
½ tsp cardamom (*elaichi*) powder
A few strands saffron (*kesar*) mixed with 1 tsp warm water
2 tbsp sliced almonds (*badam*) for the garnish

1. Combine the almonds along with ¼ cup of milk in a mixer and blend to a smooth paste. Keep aside.
2. Heat the ghee in a non-stick pan, add the almond paste and cook over a medium flame while stirring continuously till it turns light pink in colour.
3. Add the remaining milk and ¼ cup of water, mix well and simmer for 2 to 3 minutes.
4. Add the sugar, cardamom powder and saffron mixture and cook, while stirring continuously till the sugar dissolves and the ghee separates.

Serve hot garnished with almonds.

**Tips**
To blanch almonds, add the almonds to hot water and keep aside for 10 to 15 minutes. Remove, discard the skin and use as required.

Almonds boost brain power. Ensure that you include a few in your child's diet in some form. Here are some easy and sneaky ways to do so.....

- Almond milk.. Blend soaked and peeled almonds, saffron, sugar and milk for this tasty drink.
- Roasted and salted almonds.. Available readymade.
- Sugar coated almonds.....Just dip the almonds in three string sugar syrup and let it dry.
- Almond Cookies.. Ensure its home-made as the store bought ones have hardly any almonds.
- Toffee Almonds... Almonds coated with butterscotch sauce.

And if your child refuses to eat any of the above, you can always give him chocolate coated almonds.

# Mini Raisin Muffins

Homemade muffins are nutritious and can easily satisfy the craving for sweets, without all the calories of a frosted cake. Oats and raisins further add their goodness making these muffins a healthy treat for little brains. These muffins are sure to ward off all the stress your little one goes through during exams.

Nutritive values per muffin

Protein: 3.8 gm

Preparation Time: 15 minutes.   Cooking Time: Nil.   Makes 7 muffins.
Baking Temperature: 180°C (360°F).   Baking Time: 20 to 25 minutes.

¾ cup plain flour (*maida*)
¼ cup whole wheat flour (*gehun ka atta*)
¼ tsp baking powder
¼ cup butter, softened
⅓ cup sugar
1¼ cups milk
¼ tsp vanilla essence
3 tbsp quick cooking rolled oats
¼ cup chopped raisins (*kismis*)
1½ tsp fruit salt

1. Sieve the flour, wheat flour and baking powder together. Repeat again for 2 to 3 times. Keep aside.
2. Cream the butter and sugar together in a bowl till smooth and creamy.
3. Add the milk and vanilla essence and mix gently.
4. Slowly add the flour, oats and raisins and mix gently.
5. Sprinkle first the fruit salt followed by 1 tbsp of water on it and mix gently so as to incorporate air into the batter.
6. Divide the batter into 7 equal portion and spoon out each portion of the batter into 7 small paper cups and bake in a pre-heated oven at 180°C (360°F) for 15 to 20 minutes or till they turn brown. Serve hot.

## Muffin match
*Neha had a great time making these muffins. Can you tell which two are EXACTLY alike?*

(1)   (2)   (3)   (4)
(5)   (6)   (7)   (8)

# Vegetable Houses

Serve desi dalia in an international style with vegetables and cheese, and your kids are sure to fall head over heels in love with it! Pour the prepared mixture into moulds of desired shapes and sizes, for interesting visual appeal.

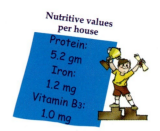

Nutritive values per house
Protein: 5.2 gm
Iron: 1.2 mg
Vitamin B$_3$: 1.0 mg

**Preparation Time: 15 minutes.   Cooking Time: 20 minutes.   Makes 4 houses.**

½ cup broken wheat (*dalia*)
1 cup milk
2 tsp butter
¼ cup chopped onions
½ tsp ginger-garlic paste (optional)
⅓ cup finely chopped mixed vegetables (carrots, corn, French beans etc.)
¼ cup grated cooking cheese
Salt and freshly ground pepper to taste
A few wafer biscuits, a few carrots cubes, and a few French bean slices for the garnish

1. Combine the broken wheat, ½ cup of milk and ½ cup of water in a non-stick pan and cook on a slow flame while stirring continuously till the broken wheat gets cooked. Remove and keep aside.
2. Heat the butter in the same pan, add the onions, ginger-garlic paste and sauté till the onions turn translucent.
3. Add the mixed vegetables and sauté for 2 more minutes.
4. Add the broken wheat mixture, remaining ½ cup milk and cook on a medium flame till the liquid evaporates, while stirring continuously.
5. Add the cheese, salt and pepper and mix well. Cook for another 2 minutes or till the cheese melts.
6. Remove from the flame and keep aside to cool.
7. When cool, divide the mixture into 4 equal portions and put each portion into a square shape cookie moulds and press it firmly. Unmould and keep aside.
8. Just before serving, make a roof using wafer biscuits, door using carrots and windows using French beans as shown in the picture. Serve immediately.

## Spot the differences

*Raja painted one beautiful house, but when he painted the same one for the second time, he made some mistakes. Help him spot those and rectify the painting.*

# Muesli Coated Fruits

Iron, required for the continuous supply of blood and nutrients to the brain and keep it functioning efficiently, which is found in applicable amounts in Muesli. Coating the fruits with luscious butterscotch sauce and serving with this crunchy muesli makes them totally irresistible. Watch the kids gobble them up!

Nutritive values per serving
Calcium: 57.9 mg
Iron: 1.3 mg

Preparation Time: 5 minutes.    Cooking Time: 10 minutes.    Serves 4.

¾ cup muesli, page 40, lightly crushed
1 small banana, cut into pieces
1 small apple, cut into pieces
1 orange, separated into segments

**For the butterscotch sauce**
½ cup sugar
2 tbsp fresh cream
¼ cup milk

**For the butterscotch sauce**
1. Heat a non-stick pan, add the sugar and allow it to caramelize to a light brown colour.
2. Remove from the flame, add the cream and milk and simmer on a slow flame to get a smooth syrup.
3. Allow it to simmer for 2 minutes till the sauce thickens. Keep aside.

**How to proceed**
1. Add the fruits to the sauce and mix well till the sauce coats each piece evenly.
2. Divide into 4 equal portions and keep aside.
3. Divide the muesli into 4 equal portions and keep aside.
4. Just before serving, place a portion of muesli in an individual serving bowl, top it with a portion of fruits and refrigerate to chill.
5. Repeat with remaining ingredients to make 3 more servings. Serve chilled.

## Breakfast Crossword

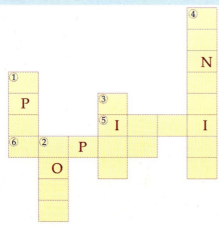

**Vertical**
1. A rawa delicacy.... ④
2. Maharashtrian's favourite... ④
3. A glassful of .... ④
4. Bread and veggie combo.... ⑧

**Horizontal**
5. Goes well with sambhar and chutney... ④
6. An _____ a day keep doctor away... ⑤

86

# Spinach Malfati

Steamed spinach dumplings served with hot tangy tomato sauce and gooey cheese makes an ideal and wholesome mini meal when served with garlic bread or rice. Both tomatoes and spinach are rich in folic acid, an important nutrient that promotes the growth and development of brain cells right from infancy till the brain is completely mature.

Nutritive values per serving
Iron: 1.0 mg
Folic Acid: 61.5 mcg

Preparation Time: 25 minutes.   Cooking Time: 25 minutes.   Serves 6.
Baking Temperature: 200°C (400°F).   Baking Time: 20 minutes.

### For the spinach dumplings
3 cups finely chopped spinach (*palak*), blanched
¾ cup crumbled *paneer* (cottage cheese)
2 pinches nutmeg (*jaiphal*) powder
2 tbsp rice flour (*chawal ka atta*)
A pinch of baking powder
Salt to taste

### For the tomato sauce
2 tsp oil
2 tsp finely chopped garlic
1 spring onion (including greens), finely chopped
1½ cups tomato pulp
1 tsp dry red chilli flakes (paprika)
½ tsp chilli powder
2 tbsp tomato purée
Salt to taste
¼ cup milk

### Other ingredients
2 tbsp grated mozzarella cheese for the topping

### For the spinach dumplings
1. Combine all the ingredients together in a bowl and mix well.
2. Divide it into small equal-sized portions and shape each portion into a ball.
3. Steam in a steamer for 5 to 7 minutes. Keep aside.

### For the tomato sauce
1. Heat the oil in a non-stick pan, add the garlic and spring onions and sauté for 1 minute.
2. Add the tomato pulp and simmer till the sauce thickens.
3. Add the chilli flakes, chilli powder, tomato purée, salt and ½ cup of water and bring to boil.
4. Add the milk, mix well and simmer for a minute. Keep aside.

### How to proceed
1. Arrange the spinach dumplings in a glass baking dish in an even layer and pour the tomato sauce over it.
2. Sprinkle the cheese on top and bake in a pre-heated oven at 200°C (400°F) for 15 minutes or till the cheese melts. Serve hot.

# Pulse Appe

A yummy south Indian snack put together with a blend of pulses that are rich in B-complex vitamins, especially vitamin $B_1$ and folic acid. Fermenting these dals increases their nutrient content making this recipe a nutritious nibble for young, growing brains.

Nutritive values per *appe*
Protein: 7.9 gm
Folic Acid: 50.3 mcg
Vitamin $B_1$: 0.2 mg

Preparation Time: 20 minutes.   Cooking Time: 40 minutes.   Makes 25 *appes*.
Soaking Time: 2 hours.   Fermenting Time: Overnight.

¾ cup *chana dal* (split Bengal gram)
¼ cup *toovar* (*arhar*) *dal*
1 tbsp green *moong dal* (split green gram)
1 tsp *urad dal* (split black gram)
½ cup parboiled rice
½ cup raw rice
½ cup chopped spinach (*palak*)
½ cup chopped fenugreek (*methi*) leaves
Salt to taste
1 tsp oil
¼ cup chopped onions
4 to 5 curry leaves (*kadi patta*)
A pinch of turmeric powder (*haldi*)
A pinch of asafoetida (*hing*)
½ tsp chilli powder
1 tbsp oil for cooking

1. Wash and soak the *dals*, parboiled rice and raw rice in lukewarm water for at least 2 hours.
2. Drain and put the *dals* and rice in a mixer and blend to a smooth paste using little water if required. Cover and keep aside overnight.
3. Next day, add enough water to get a batter of dropping consistency.
4. Add the spinach, fenugreek and salt and mix well. Keep aside.
5. For the tempering, heat the oil in a small non-stick pan, add the onions and sauté till the onions turns light brown.
6. Add the curry leaves, turmeric powder, asafoetida and chilli powder and sauté for another minute.
7. Pour the tempering over the batter and mix well. Keep aside.
8. Heat the *appe* moulds on a medium flame and grease it with a little oil.
9. Pour a spoonful of the batter into each mould and cook till the outer surface becomes golden brown and then turn each *appe* upside down using a fork so as to cook on the other side.
10. Repeat with the remaining batter to make more *appes*.
Serve hot.

### Appe Mould

Appe moulds are easily available in the market in the iron and non-stick variety.

# Paneer Papad Kurkure

Chilli-garlic paneer potato balls, dipped in batter, coated with coarsely ground papad, and deep-fried till crisp. Just a description of this dish is enough to make your kids drool over it. Ideal protein-rich snack to serve when your kids take a break while studying for the exams!

Nutritive values per *kurkure*
Energy: 94 kcal
Protein: 2.6 gm

Preparation Time: 5 minutes.   Cooking Time: 15 minutes.   Makes 10 *kurkures*.

2 *papads*, raw
1 cup grated *paneer* (cottage cheese)
2 tbsp tomato ketchup
½ tbsp schezwan sauce
¼ cup boiled and mashed potatoes
Salt to taste
¼ cup plain flour (*maida*) mixed with ¼ cup water
Oil for deep-frying

1. Grind the *papads* in a mixer to a powder and keep aside.
2. Combine the *paneer*, tomato ketchup, schezwan sauce, potatoes and salt and mix well.
3. Divide the mixture into 10 equal portions and shape each portion into a ball.
4. Dip each ball in the flour mixture and roll them in the powdered *papads*.
5. Heat the oil in a *kadhai* and deep-fry the sandwiched *paneer* cubes till they turn golden brown in colour.
6. Drain on an absorbent paper and serve hot.

## Other munchie ideas for kids during exams to keep them energetic all through the day:

- **Caramel Popcorn** : Heat a non-stick pan, add the sugar and cook till it caramelises (turn golden brown in colour), add the popcorn and toss well. You can also add nuts along with popcorn for a nutritious treat.

- **Carrot and Cheese Sandwiches** : Quick to assemble, just combine grated carrots, grated cheese, salt, pepper and mayonnaise (if you kid likes) together. Stuff this mixture in between buttered brown bread slices to make a filling sandwich.

- **Date and Nut Balls** : To make this sweet and a healthy treat in a jiffy, heat the ghee in a non-stick pan, add the seedless dates and cook till they become soft, add the roasted nuts (almonds, cashewnuts, walnuts etc), mix well and shape into balls.

- **Spinach and Paneer Kurkure** : Mash the *paneer*, add shredded spinach, bread crumbs, salt, green chillies and mix well. Shape this mixture into balls, roll them in crushed *papads* and deep-fry till golden brown. *Kurkure* is ready!

- **Corn and Potato Kurkure** : Use mashed potatoes and boiled sweet corn instead of *paneer* and spinach and follow the procedure given above to make my variation of *kurkure*.

# Labneh with Crispy Vegetables

Help your kids face exams bravely! This nutritious recipe will help overcome examination fear and anxiety. Brimming with protein, calcium and folic acid, serve this to your kids on a tense evening before exams, or even during parties!

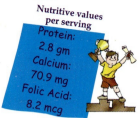

**Nutritive values per serving**
Protein: 2.8 gm
Calcium: 70.9 mg
Folic Acid: 8.2 mcg

Preparation Time: 20 minutes.  Cooking Time: 5 minutes.  Serves 4.

**For the crispy vegetables**
1 cup thinly sliced rounds of mixed vegetables (carrots, baby corn, zucchini, potatoes, small brinjals etc.)
½ cup cornflour
Salt to taste
Oil for deep-frying

**To be blended into labneh**
½ cup thick hung curds *(chakka dahi)*
2 tsp fresh cream
1 clove garlic, grated
1 tbsp tomato ketchup
1 tbsp chopped coriander *(dhania)*
Salt to taste

**For the crispy vegetables**
1. Spread ¼ cup of sliced vegetables on a flat plate and sprinkle 2 tbsp of cornflour and salt over it and mix well.
2. Heat the oil in a *kadhai* on a medium flame and deep-fry the vegetables till golden brown and crisp. Drain on an absorbent paper.
3. Repeat steps 1 and 2 to make 3 more servings of crispy vegetables.

**How to serve**
Serve the crispy vegetables immediately with the prepared labneh.

# Orange Banana Smoothie

Kids love variety in everything. How can they not be impressed by a recipe that packs a dazzling variety of flavours into every single sip! Oranges are tart, bananas are sweet and fresh curds whipped together are sure to steal your child's heart and meet their calcium and protein needs just in a glass.

**Nutritive values per glass**
Protein: 5.1 gm
Calcium: 225.3 mg

Preparation Time: 5 minutes.   Cooking Time: Nil.   Makes 4 glasses.

½ cup peeled orange segments
¾ cup chopped bananas
1½ cups thick fresh curds (*dahi*)
½ cup milk
2 tsp powdered sugar
4 ice-cubes

1. Combine all the ingredients and blend in a mixer till smooth.
2. Pour into 4 individual glasses and serve immediately.

# Answers

Page No.

**22  Make the picture**
*Telephone*

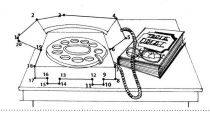

**26  Pave a Path**

**30  Oodles of Noodles**

**46  Yummy Toppings**
*a. Butter*
*b. Jam*
*c. Cheese*

**52  "P" Pyramid**
*1. Pea*
*2. Pour*
*3. Plate*
*4. Pepper*
*5. Preheat*

**56  Find the missing food**
*SweeTlime*
*PIneapple*
*Kiwi*
*ChicKoo*
*FIgs*          **TIKKI**

**74  Make your own bhel**
*Sev*
*Peanuts*
*Puri*
*Tomatoes*
*Puffed rice*
*Onions*
*Lemon*
*Chutney*

Page No.

**82  Muffin match**   *4th and 6th are alike*

**84  Spot the differences**   *7 mistakes*

**86  Breakfast Crossword**

**Vertical**
1. Upma
2. Poha
3. Milk
4. Sandwich

**Horizontal**
5. Idli
6. Apple